COLLINS
GEM

BASIC FACTS

COMPUTERS

Brian Samways
BSc MInstP

Collins
London and Glasgow

First published 1983
Reprint 10 9 8 7

© William Collins Sons & Co. Ltd. 1983

ISBN 0 00 458890 8

Author Brian Samways
Series Editor Ken Davison
Assistants Trevor Cross Tony Byrne-Jones

Phototypeset and Illustrated by
Parkway Illustrated Press

Printed in Great Britain by
Collins Clear-Type Press, Glasgow

Introduction

Basic Facts is a new generation of illustrated GEM dictionaries in important school subjects. They cover all the important ideas and topics in these subjects up to the level of first examinations.

Bold words in an entry mean a word or idea is developed further in a separate entry.

A full list of acronyms (alphabetically arranged) is given at the front of the dictionary. These are used throughout the text.

Abbreviations, Acronyms and Meaningful Words

A

ACARD	Advisory Council for Applied Research and Development
ACE	Automatic Computing Engine (1950)
A/D	Analogue to Digital
ADA	A programming language
ADP	Automatic Data Processing
ALGOL	ALGOrithmic Language
ALU	Arithmetic Logic Unit
AND	A Logic Gate
APL	A Programming Language
ASCC	Automatic Sequence Controlled Calculator (1944)
ASCII	American Standard Code for Information Interchange

B

BASIC	Beginner's All-purpose Symbolic Instruction Code
BBC	British Broadcasting Corporation
BCD	Binary Coded Decimal
BCS	British Computer Society
BIT	Binary DigIT
BLAISE	British Library Automated Information Service
BSI	British Standards Institute

C

CAD	Computer Aided Design
CAI	Computer Assisted Instruction
CAL	Computer Assisted Learning
CAM	Computer Aided Manufacture
CBL	Computer Based Learning
CBT	Computer Based Training
CCD	Charge Coupled Device
CDT	Craft Design Technology
CMI	Computer Managed Instruction
CML	Computer Managed Learning
CMOS	Complementary MOS
COBOL	Common Business Oriented Language
COM	Computer Output on Microfilm
COMAL	High level programming language
CORAL	High level programming language
CP/M	Control Program for Microcomputer
CPS	Characters Per Second
CPU	Central Processing Unit
CRT	Cathode-Ray Tube

D

DETAB	A programming language
DOS	Disk Operating System
DP	Data Processing
DTL	Diode Transistor Logic

E

EAROM	Electrically Alterable ROM
EBCDIC	Extended Binary Coded Decimal Interchange Code
ECMA	European Computer Manufacturers' Association
EDP	Electronic Data Processing
EDSAC	Electronic Delay Storage Automatic Computer (1949)
EDVAC	Electrical Discrete Variable Automatic Computer (1949)
ELSI	Extra Large Scale Integration
ENIAC	Electronic Numerical Integrator And Calculator (1946)
EPROM	Erasable Programmable Read Only Memory

F

FET	Field Effect Transistor
FORTRAN	FORmula TRANslation
FM	Frequency Modulation

G

| GIGO | Garbage In Garbage Out |

H

| HZ | Hertz |

IAL	International Algebraic Language
IAR	Instruction Address Register
IAS	Immediate Access Store
IBA	Independent Broadcasting Authority
IBM	International Business Machines
IC	Integrated Circuit
ICL	International Computers Limited
IDP	Integrated Data Processing
IEE	Institute of Electrical Engineers
IEEE	A standard interface
IFIP	International Federation for Information Processing
INTELSAT	INternational TELecommunications SATellite consortium
I/O	Input and Output
IP	Information Provider
ISBN	International Standard Book Number
ISO	International Organisation for **Standardisation**

J

| JCL | Job Control Language |

K

| K | Kilo or 1000 but 1024 in computer storage locations |

L

LCD	Liquid Crystal Display
LED	Light Emitting Diode
LEO	Lyons Electronic Office (1951)
LPM	Lines Per Minute
LSE	Language Symbolique d'Enseignement
LSI	Large Scale Integration

M

MAP	Microprocessor Application Project
MENTOR	A CBL system
MICR	Magnetic Ink Character Recognition
MISP	Microelectronics Industry Support Programme
MODEM	Modulator-Demonstrator
MOS	Metal Oxide Semiconductor
MOSFET	Metal Oxide Semiconductor Field Effect Transistor
MPU	Microprocessor Unit
MSI	Medium Scale Integration

N

NAND	A Not AND Logic Gate
NCC	National Computing Centre
NEQ	A Non-Equivalence Logic Gate
NOR	A Not OR Logic Gate
NOT	A Logic Gate

O

OCR	Optical Character Recognition
OEM	Original Equipment Manufacturer
OPAMP	Operational Amplifier
OP-CODE	Operation Code
OR	A Logic Gate

P

PAL	Phase Alternation line (A colour TV system)
PASCAL	High level programming language
PCB	Printed Circuit Board
PIXEL	PICture ELements
PILOT	An author language
PIO	Programmable Input/Output
PL/1	Programming Language 1
PLATO	A CBL system
PROM	Programmable Read Only Memory

Q

QWERTY	The normal typewriter keyboard

R

RAM	Random Access Memory
RF	Radio Frequency
RGB	Red, Green, Blue
RJE	Remote Job Entry
ROM	Read Only Memory
RS232	A standard serial interface
RS423	A standard serial interface
RTL	Resistor Transistor Logic

S

S100	A standard bus
SSI	Small Scale Integration

T

TRL	Transistor Resistor Logic
TTL	Transistor Transistor Logic

U

UHF	Ultra High Frequency
ULA	Uncommitted Logic Array
UNIVAC	Universal Automatic Computer (1951)

V

VDU	Visual Display Unit
VHF	Very High Frequency
VLF	Very Low Frequency
VLSI	Very Large Scale Integration

W

WP	Word Processor

X

X–Y	Two directions at right angles

Abacus One of the first gadgets for doing arithmetic, used for addition and subtraction. It has ten balls or beads in each row if working in **denary**. Multiplication and division are carried out by repeated addition and subtraction just as in calculators and computers today. Another similarity is that it stores the result as well as doing the calculation. An advanced type is still used in parts of China as a cheap, easy-to-use calculating device and is very fast in the hands of an expert.

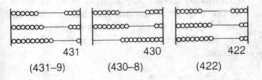

| 431 | 430 | 422 |
| (431–9) | (430–8) | (422) |

For example: to calculate 431–9, note that ten beads on one row can be exchanged for one ball on the row above at any time during a calculation.

Abort In the same way as the count-down of a space-launch is sometimes stopped so the running of a computer program is made to cease when things go wrong. In both cases we would use the word abort, though in the computer case we would return to the **operating system** after aborting the program. Here the computer would print a message and wait for a command.

Absolute Address To visit a friend you need to find the house, and you can do this if you have the address. **Data** held in a computer is found by giving the address of its location. When we program in **machine code** the number given to each address is governed by the **hardware** and is called the absolute address.

Access Time Is the time taken by the computer to fetch **data** from an **address** within the computer or other storage device. The time between being told to fetch and having the data ready.

Accumulator A special **location** used to store the answer when doing arithmetic. The accumulator, on being given a number, can add it to the number already held and then hold the result.

For example: a program in **machine code** designed to add two numbers together would carry out the arithmetic with three instructions

Accumulator

| 0 | → | 37 | → | 85 |

a) clear accumulator
b) transfer first number to accumulator (37)
c) add second number to accumulator (48)

Acoustic Coupler A communications device into which fits a telephone handset. Digital signals using **serial transmission** can then be sent from or to a computer via the telephone system. Two tones (i.e. two different sounds) are used, one for 0's and one for 1's.

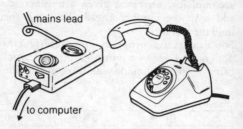

mains lead

to computer

Acronym The world of computing has many acronyms. These consist of a simple set of letters taken from the letters of a word or phrase.

For example: **BASIC** is an acronym for **Be-ginners' All-purpose Symbolic Instruction Code** and it is much easier to say 'BASIC'.

There is a list of acronyms at the beginning of the book.

Adder A device which performs addition on digital signals giving both the sum and the carry digit. A **half-adder** has two inputs each of which can be a 0 or 1 whereas a full-adder has three inputs.

For example: when adding two binary numbers together electronically the first column on the right can be dealt with by a **half-adder** but the other columns require a full-adder as there is a carry digit from the previous column.

$$1001101$$
$$+0110111$$
$$\overline{10000100}$$

Address A computer stores **data** and so that it can be found each store-**location** has an address.

For example:

address	contents
140	C
141	A
142	T
143	255

Address 142 holds the letter T, though both would be stored in **binary notation**. Just as the word CAT is held in three locations so more than one location can be used to hold a number.

Address Bus A major route (set of wires) along which signals travel to indicate a particular **address**. **Data** can then be put into or taken from that address along the **data bus**.

Address Modification This is a process by which the address part of a program instruction is changed, say to one higher (i.e. the next address) each time the instruction is performed.

For example: this is very useful if a series of inputs are to be placed in consecutive addresses.

Aiken Howard Aiken, an American, realised the importance of Babbage's **analytical engine** and suggested the Automatic Sequence Controlled Calculator (ASCC) which, built in the mid 1940's, was the first automatic computer. The program instructions were supplied to this electromechanical machine on paper tape.

Algol (acronym for **ALGO**rithmic **L**anguage) a high level programming language developed in Europe at the same time as

FORTRAN was being developed in the United States. ALGOL60 is a problem-solving language designed for mathematical and scientific use whereas ALGOL68 is an even more powerful language designed in 1968 for a variety of uses.

Algorithm A set of instructions or steps that one plans in order to find a method for solving a problem. There is only one starting point and all routes through the algorithm end at the same finishing point. Such steps can be carried out by a computer (or human) using different inputs or values.

Alphanumeric Code A set of characters consisting of the letters A to Z and numbers 0 to 9.
For example: an alphanumeric keyboard.

(1) (2) (3) (4) (5) (6) (7) (8) (9) (0)

(Q) (W) (E) (R) (T) (Y) (U) (I) (O) (P)

(A) (S) (D) (F) (G) (H) (J) (K) (L)

(Z) (X) (C) (V) (B) (N) (M)

Amplifier A device that accepts a varying electrical signal and is capable of making its voltage (or the current) bigger.

Analogue Computer This is a machine designed to work on **data** which is represented by some physical quantity which varies continuously (unlike digital signals which are 0's and 1's).

For example: the turning of a wheel or changes in voltage can be used as input. Analogue computers are said to operate in **real time** because they respond as things happen and are widely used for research in design where many different shapes and speeds can be tried out quickly. A computer model of a car suspension allows the designer to see the effects of changing size, stiffness and damping.

Analytical Engine The first machine designed to carry out complicated arithmetical tasks. Invented in 1833 by the Englishman Charles **Babbage** it was ahead of its time as the engineers could not make all the necessary parts to the required accuracy. The mechanical forerunner of today's computer.

AND Gate This is a logic gate which operates with **binary digits**. Its output is of logic value 1 only when all its inputs have a logic value 1.

For example: with a two input AND gate the following **truth table** applies.

an AND gate

Input		Output
0	0	0
0	1	0
1	0	0
1	1	1

This could be used to find the carry digit when two binary digits are added together as there is a carry of 1 only when the two digits to be added are both 1's.

Applications Package   The name given to a program or set of programs written to carry out a specific task.

For example: a wages or payroll package
a warehouse-control program
a program controlling a robot welder

Archived File   As the name suggests this type of file is kept, say, on magnetic tape and has to be loaded on to the disk or tape drive when required. It is not kept permanently in the computer and so does not take up valuable space.

Argument   A variable factor, the value of which sets the value of the function of which it is part.

For example: to find the square root when programming in **BASIC** we use a function such as SQR(X). The value of this function is governed by the value of the argument X.

Arithmetic Logic Unit (ALU)   This is the part of the computer where the calculations are carried out (addition and subtraction) and

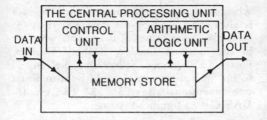

THE CENTRAL PROCESSING UNIT

CONTROL UNIT

ARITHMETIC LOGIC UNIT

DATA IN

DATA OUT

MEMORY STORE

the logic operations are performed. The ALU is part of the **central processing unit** and has an arithmetic register for holding the results of calculations during processing.

Array The name given to an arranged set of locations any of which can be accessed from a common starting address rather than individually.

For example: consider a block of flats having eight floors with four flats on each floor. The flats could be numbered (coded) 1 to 32 as in a one-dimensional array and referred to as FLAT 1, FLAT 2 etc. Alternatively they could be numbered 11 to 14 on the first level, 21 to 24 on the second level, 31 to 34 on the third level as in a two–dimensional array and referred to as LEVEL 2 ROOM 3 etc. (Note that when using rows and columns an item of **data** is always accessed by the row and then the column). If the names of the people who live in the flats are Oakley, Talbot, Thomas, Foster, Fish, Simons, Selby, Ellis, Nelson and so on, then these names could be stored in a one-dimensional array F$1, F$2, F$3, etc. (In **BASIC** the $ signifies a **string**)

F$(1)	Oakley
F$(2)	Talbot
F$(3)	Thomas
F$(4)	Foster
F$(5)	Fish

However a two-dimensional array is more convenient when dealing with large amounts of **data**.

1st level	Oakley	Talbot	Thomas	Foster
2nd level	Fish	Simons	Selby	Ellis

To obtain the names of those living at the seventh level we would use references F$(7,1), F$(7,2), F$(7,3) and F$(7,4).

Artificial Intelligence This is the name used to describe the ability of a machine to learn from its experiences and to make decisions based on these experiences, rather like a human being.

For example: a machine may play chess, but if each time it plays it learns from its mistakes and plays better the next time, then it is said to have artificial intelligence.

ASCII code (acronym for **A**merican **S**tandard **C**ode for **I**nformation **I**nterchange – pronounced 'ASKEY') A standard code used for

Characters and their ASCII code

0	48	C	67	O	79	a	97
1	49	D	68	P	80	b	98
2	50	E	69	Q	81	c	99
3	51	F	70	R	82	d	100
4	52	G	71	S	83	e	101
5	53	H	72	T	84	space	32
6	54	I	73	U	85	!	33
7	55	J	74	V	86	*	42
8	56	K	75	W	87	+	43
9	57	L	76	X	88	–	45
A	65	M	77	Y	89	/	47
B	66	N	78	Z	90	=	61

the transmission of **data**; particularly the exchange of data between machines. Many manufacturers design their own codes for their machines but ASCII code is often used as a standard thus enabling link-ups between various computers and **peripherals** such as **printers**.

Aspect Ratio   The ratio of the width of a television picture to the height. 4:3 has been adopted by the United Kingdom and many other countries.

Assembly Language   This is a **low level language** which is similar to the way in which the computer hardware works but is easier to use than machine code for programming. The computer manufacturer provides an **Assembler** and this program translates the completed assembly language program into **machine code**; one programming instruction becoming one machine code instruction.

Assign   This is reserving part of the computing system, say the printer, for use by a program during its running. Note that 'allocate' is similar but is controlled during the running and may make the particular hardware available to other programs at certain times.

Astable An electronic device which has two states but is continually switching from one to the other. It is used as the timing device in electronic watches and as the basis for the computer **clock**.

Asynchronous Mode The way in which a computer works whereby the end of one operation allows the start of the next. The machine does not have to wait for the next **clock** cycle to start each operation as in **synchronous mode**.

Atlas The best-known of the **second generation** computers which were built using **transistors** as opposed to the thermionic **valves** of the **first generation**.

A to D Converter (analogue to digital) A device that is able to convert a continuously varying signal, such as voltage, into a series of numbers. It does this by sampling the voltage at regular intervals (ten times a second say) and changing its digital output accordingly.

For example: when a computer is used to switch on and off a heating system it must be able to measure the temperature. Electrical thermometers provide varying voltages (analogue) which have to be converted into a series of digits (a binary number) for the computer.

Author Language   The name given to a programming language that allows the user to have little or no knowledge of programming. With an author language the non-computer specialist can compose a learning sequence in a particular subject for his own students.
For example: **PILOT**.

Automatic Computing Engine (ACE)
The fastest of the early computers built in 1950 by the National Physics Laboratory. Parts can still be seen in the London Science Museum.

Auto-start   With some commercial microcomputers an auto-start code is stored in **read-only-memory** (ROM). In such cases on switching on this automatically loads, say, the **BASIC interpreter** and a program into the machine which is then immediately ready for use.

Babbage   Charles Babbage (English 1791–1871). He saw the need for an accurate calculating device and tried to build his 'difference engine'. In 1833 he proposed the **analytical engine** which in principle was the forerunner of today's computer. Using punched cards it was designed to perform calculations automatically and was the first type of digital computer.

Backing Store   A store for large amounts of **data** which can be transmitted easily (though not always quickly) to the **main store** when required. It also has the advantage of being a non-**volatile memory**.
For example: magnetic card or magnetic disk.

Backup   Designed to provide a service when things go wrong. Should a set of records become corrupt then this allows one to start again with the original **data**.
For example: in keeping records on a **disk** for a **microcomputer** one should keep three copies. Should one disk become damaged during updating, the operator can continue with the next copy knowing that there is still a third

copy. If there were only two copies and the first was damaged, then the second has to be duplicated on to another disk before being **updated** and this could result in the updated records being lost whilst the second disk is being copied. The third copy is always stored separately from the first two.

Bar Code   These consist of a set of lines of varying widths which can be read by passing a **light pen** across them. On household goods there are 30 lines giving a unique 13-digit code number to each product. On being recorded by the cashier, the machine finds the price from **memory** and is able to record the fact that there is now one less of that item in stock.

ISBN 0-00-616496-X

9 780006 164968

Library cards and library books sometimes have bar codes, though with more lines. Here the borrowing of books during the day is recorded on to tape using a light pen (bar code scanner) and the **data** transferred to the computer at the end of the day.

BASIC (acronym for **B**eginner's **A**ll-purpose **S**ymbolic **I**nstruction **C**ode) A **high level** programming **language** used for general or conversational programming. Developed by Kemeny and Kurtz in 1964 in the USA, it was originally designed for educational use as an easy-to-learn language. Students could input their programs one line at a time each of which would be checked by the computer before the next one would be accepted.

Batch Processing The system of collecting all the different inputs or **programs** together and putting them into a computer in one set or a batch. This only involves the operator in 'one' loading and running operation no matter how many programs are in the batch. The programs are processed as a single unit thus avoiding wasted computer time as each program is loaded.

For example: in a school without its own computing facilities each pupil in a class could write a program on **mark sense cards** and these could be taken and fed, on batch, to a distant computer. Not only would there usually be a delay before these are run but several days could pass before the output was returned.

Baud Rate Named after the Frenchman, Baudot, this rate today is taken as the number of **bits** per second transmitted along a wire. Originally it was based on the speeds of transmitting the morse code.

Rate	Used by
110 baud	Teletype terminal to computer
300 baud	Slow-speed cassette tape to micro
1200 baud	Prestel set receiving data
7000000 baud	Data transfer by satellites
1000 million baud	Possible speed with **optic fibre**

Benchmark A program task which is given to different makes of computers to measure their performance thus enabling a comparison to be made.

Binary Coded Decimal (BCD) To be able to change any of our numbers 0 to 9 into binary, we require up to four **binary digits**. The coding system BCD uses four binary digits for each decimal number.

decimal	binary code
0	0000
1	0001
2	0010
3	0011
4	0100
5	0101
6	0110
7	0111
8	1000
9	1001

denary	binary	hex
10	1010	A
11	1011	B
12	1100	C
13	1101	D
14	1110	E
15	1111	F

But note that with four binary digits numbers up to 15 can be coded in this way. The final six numbers are coded as letters in the **hexadecimal** system.

Binary Digit Either a 0 or 1. It is one of the two digits used in **binary notation**.

Binary Fractions Each **binary digit** has twice the value of the one on its right whether it comes before or after the bicimal point.
For example: 11.11 in binary represents $2 + 1 + \frac{1}{2} + \frac{1}{4} = 3.75$ in **denary**.

Binary Notation In this system numbers are represented by the two digits 0 and 1, i.e. base 2.

Binary	Denary		Binary	Denary
0	0		101	5
1	1		110	6
10	2		111	7
11	3		1000	8
100	4			

and so on.

When we count in tens (base 10) each digit is ten times the value of the one on its right. In binary (base 2) each digit has twice the value. For example: 10011 in binary is 19 in denary.

16	8	4	2	1
1	0	0	1	1

$$16 + 0 + 0 + 2 + 1 = 19$$

Using the same rules as for denary arithmetic

binary addition	binary subtraction
0010	1101
+1011	−0110
1101	0111

but see **complement**.

Binary notation having only two digits can be easily represented electronically by two voltage levels and can be stored in any system having two states. For these reasons it is used by computers.

24

Bistable An electronic device which has two states and is the basis of a computer memory. In one state it can be considered to represent a 0 and in the other state a 1.

Bit One of the two digits 0 and 1 used in **binary notation**. The word comes from BInary digiT.

Black Box A concept used to understand how units go together to make a system without having to understand the workings of the individual units.

For example: a public address system may be considered to be just three black boxes.

Microphone → Amplifier → Loudspeaker

and the amplifier itself as three black boxes

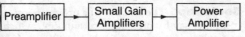

Preamplifier → Small Gain Amplifiers → Power Amplifier

Block A set of records, figures or words which are treated by the computer as a single unit of **data**.

For example: **microcomputer** data is trans-

25

ferred to and from a cassette tape recorder in blocks. These blocks are sometimes indicated by numbers on the screen though can be distinctly heard by just playing the tape.

Block Diagram This is a diagram used to help explain a system and consists of labelled boxes joined by lines with arrows similar to a program **flowchart** and it is used for systems such as electrical circuits.

For example:

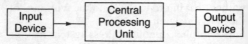

Boolean Algebra First presented to the world in 1847 by George Boole this set of rules allows logical statements to be written using algebra. The results of such statements can be shown in a **truth table**.

Bootstrap The loading of a program into a computer say by pressing a certain key, which first calls in routines which have to be used to load programs. Switching on a computer does not mean that it is ready – 'booting' the system normally gives the user some form of **operating system**.

Branch A computer carries out each program step in turn but can be made to jump to a different part of the program by a branch instruction.

For example: a conditional branch might depend on the value of something at that time, i.e. branch if the value of X is greater than 7. **Structured programming** avoids the use of the branch.

Breadboard An experimental circuit board which is used to try out possible circuits. Often included on a **microprocessor** learning/teaching kit for **interfacing** and control technology.

Bubble Memory Used for storing **data** in **binary notation**. Small cylinders of magnetism, called bubbles, are created and held

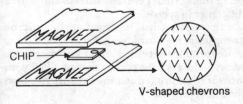

V-shaped chevrons

stationary by magnets in a **chip** made from magnetic material. Each bubble is used to represent a 1 whereas the absence of a bubble indicates a 0.

To keep the bubbles in place chevrons are put on the surface of the chip (shown V-shaped in the inset diagram). Bubbles are created at one end, moved by magnetic fields (not shown in diagram) across the chip as required and read in sequence. Thus it is a **serial access memory** but has the advantage of being non-**volatile** and capable of high density storage. This whole book could be stored as 0's and 1's on four bubble memory chips each less than a square centimetre.

Buffer A temporary store for data which is being transferred, generally used to allow for a difference in speeds.

For example: what is typed on a **micro-computer** keyboard is generally held in a buffer until the return or input key is pressed. Many **printers** have buffers that are filled with what is to be printed at a much faster rate than the actual printing.

Bug A mistake in a program or an error in the working of the computer. (An undefined extra facility).

Bus A route around the computer consisting of a set of wires along which signals travel in parallel. These signals can start from any place on the bus and can travel to any destination.

For example: in a microcomputer the **address bus** would carry signals to select a particular storage location; the **data bus** may then carry signals to transfer data to that location.

Byte A set of **binary digits**, usually representing one character, which are treated by the computer as one unit. (As many microcomputers today use an 8-bit byte structure, a byte is generally accepted to be 8 bits: a nibble being 4 bits and a slice being 1 bit).

For example: some computers use 32-bit

words with 8-bit character codes (8-bit bytes) or 18-bit words with 6-bit character codes (6-bit bytes). In the latter case each of the characters would be coded using six binary digits. Letter A might be 100001, C might be 100011 and T, 110100. Thus a three-character message would be coded as:

100011100001110100

and this is treated as an 18-bit word. Larger messages require more than one word. In this case 6 bits make 1 byte and 3 bytes make one word.

Calculator A machine which is able to do arithmetic (add, subtract, multiply and divide) and other logical operations. A programmable calculator is one which carries out a set of arithmetical operations in order according to a program. Even early calculators that worked with **punched cards** were able to follow simple programs though were not able to change their own programs or do repeated loops and branching.

Card Punch A machine that punches holes in cards so that the cards store data which can be used at a later time. When **on line** the holes are punched by signals from the computer (300 cards per minute say): **off line** they are punched by hand.

Card Reader This machine reads cards which have been prepared by the **card punch**. The data stored on the cards is taken and put in another form (e.g. electrical signals) which can be used by a computer or other device. Reading speeds of over 1000 cards per minute are possible.

Cassette Tape A cheap form of **backup** storage used with **microcomputers**. It has the advantage of being readily available (same as that used in cassette tape recorders) but is somewhat slow (between 300 and 1200 **baud**) in transferring **data**. Note that most microcomputer programs can be stored on one side of a ten-minute tape; i.e. a C10 tape.

Cathode-Ray Tube (CRT) This is the normal television picture tube and is used in **monitors** and **visual display units**. Its big advantage over the new flat screens is it superior brightness.

Ceefax The name of the BBC's **teletext** service which transmits **data** along with the normal programme transmissions. With a teletext decoder this data can be made to fill the screen (or be superimposed over the picture) one page at a time. The **data** from page 700 onwards when loaded into particular **microcomputers** provides **software** for those machines. Software transmitted thus is called **telesoftware**.

Central Processing Unit (CPU) The brains or nerve centre of a computer. It has three parts; its own store, an **arithmetic logic**

unit and a **control unit**. The control unit carries out each instruction of a program in turn. This may involve arithmetic operations being carried out on **data** being held or the moving of data from one part of the computer to another. The central processing unit is sometimes known as the Central Processor.

Charge Coupled Device (CCD) A **volatile** storage device built on a **chip** which uses a region of charge (extra electrons) to store the **binary digit** '1' and neutral regions for '0'. It needs to be continually 'refreshed' to hold the charge and when the power is switched off it loses the **data** being held.

Character A symbol used for communicating. Can be a digit (0,1,2 ...), a letter (A,B,C, ...), a punctuation mark (!,',?, ...), a sign ($\star$,+,−, ...) or just a space.

Character Code The binary code used by computers to represent **characters**. Each machine often has its own character code though there are some standard codes like **ASCII**.

Character Recognition Whereas computers can understand dots and punched holes, humans can read **characters**. To input characters into a computer one can use a keyboard to provide **character codes** though it would be much quicker if the computer could recognise written or printed characters. **Optical character recognition** (OCR) and **Magnetic ink character recognition** (MICR) are the two main systems of automatically recognising characters.

Chart Recorder A record-keeping device that plots graphs by the movement of a pen to the right or left as a piece of paper is moved steadily in one direction underneath.

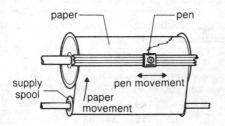

Check Digit   Used as a method of validating **data** entry. This digit is put on the end of a number or **string** of **characters** to confirm that there has not been a change whilst being transferred either by hand or wire.

For example: Consider the ISBN number of this book; the last digit is in fact a check digit.

$$\boxed{0\ 00\ 458890-?}$$

0 this gives the country (0 England, 2 Germany),

00 this is the publisher (Collins being the first),

458 used by Collins for the department code,

890 used by Collins for list number within the department.

? the check digit calculated from the previous six digits by multiplying the first by 7, the next by 6 and so on, and then adding up the totals, dividing by 11 and subtracting the remainder from 11.

$$\boxed{4\ 5\ 8\ 8\ 9\ 0}$$

$$
\begin{aligned}
& 4\times7 + 5\times6 + 8\times5 + 8\times4 + 9\times3 + 0\times2 \\
=\ & 28 + \ 30 + \ 40 + \ 32 + \ 27 + \ \ 0\ = \ 157
\end{aligned}
$$

$$157 \div 11 = 14 \text{ r } 3$$
$$11 - 3 = 8$$

Thus the ISBN number is $\boxed{0\ 00\ 458890-8}$

36

Chip A common name for **integrated circuit**.

Clock An electronic device that provides pulses at fixed time intervals. These pulses can be used to control the operations of a computer so that they are all in step (**synchronous**). Clock pulses are generated by an **astable** multivibrator.

Coaxial Cable A cable having two or more conducting wires each surrounding the one before though insulated from it. The outer conductor is usually 'earthed' so that the signals carried cannot be affected by external electric fields such as those generated by switching off a room light. Often used to connect a microcomputer to a television set or monitor.

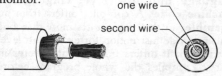

one wire

second wire

COBOL (acronym for **CO**mmon **B**usiness **O**riented **L**anguage) A world-wide **high**

level language developed in America in 1959 for general commercial programming. It has the advantage of using everyday English and is the most widely used of all the programming languages.

Code A term used to describe a set of programming instructions for a computer though may also refer to the binary patterns used to represent **characters**.

Colour Decoder An electronic device that converts coded digital signals into a form which can be used to add colour to the monitor screen. Without such a device the screen would show just two colours, usually black and white.

Compiler A program which converts computer instructions written in a **high level language** into **low level language** or **machine code**. A compiler differs from an **assembler** in that it generates more than one machine code instruction for every high level instruction. It differs from an **interpreter** in that it compiles the whole program before running. Thus one uses the compiled version of a program which is probably stored separately to the original or **source program**. It is virtually impossible for the user of a compiled program to make any changes to the program itself. Note that running times are much faster than when using an interpreter.

Complement Most commonly used is **two's complement** (the true complement) as a method of carrying out subtraction. When working with positive and negative binary numbers the leftmost **bit** is used to indicate the sign; 0 for positive, 1 for negative. However with a 1 only the first bit is negative. A decimal +6 would be expressed as 0110 in 4-bit binary whereas a decimal −6 would be expressed as 1010.

```
0110 --- (0×8+−1×4+1×2+0×1) = +6
1010 --- (1×−8+0×4+1×2+0×1) = −6
```

Thus 1010 is the two's complement of 0110. Such complements can be found by '**negation** plus one'.
For example: $7 - 6 = 1$. What is $0111 - 0110$?

$$7- \quad 6 = \quad 7 + \quad (-6) = \quad 1$$
$$0111 - 0110 = 0111 + (1010) = 10001 = 0001$$
as we are only in 4-bit binary.

Computer A machine which in a fraction of a second can produce enough errors to keep eight men occupied for the whole of their lifetime. More seriously, a machine that has three components

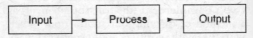

where the input and output may be **digital** or **analogue** and the process would involve storage, control and arithmetical operations. A computer differs from a **calculator** in that it automatically carries out the three operations under the control of a program. A microcomputer has a **microprocessor** as its **central processing unit.**

Computer Assisted Learning   (CAL)
Computer Based Training   (CBT)
Computer Managed Learning   (CML)
These three entries refer to the use of the computer in education, the middle word in each case defining the use. Note the other variations listed in the abbreviations section at the beginning of the book. In the case of CAL the computer could display various pieces of

information and ask particular questions depending on responses given by the user, thus assisting with the understanding of a topic. CBT uses the computer as a medium for the training course whereas with CML the computer not only provides the course but directs the student from one section to another according to his progress and records the standards attained.

Computer Bureau A company which sells time on its computer to many users. Thus a small firm can have the use of a large expensive computer quite cheaply, and in addition have the help of the bureau if needed.

Configuration This word refers to the pieces of **hardware** that make up the computer system.

(a)   monitor

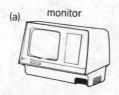

(b)
microcomputer

(c)
printer

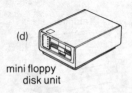

(d)
mini floppy
disk unit

For example: a common micro configuration might consist of a microcomputer with 32K **RAM**, a mini **floppy disk** of capacity 144K, a black and white **monitor** and a thermal **printer** plus the necessary connecting leads.

Console This is what the computer operator uses and may be a **visual display unit** or a typewriter keyboard. It could consist of a set of lamps with switches as this would still allow the operator to control the computer.

Continuous Stationery Paper, which may already have some printing, consisting of hundreds of perforated sheets which can be automatically fed through a printer by the **sprocket holes** along the sides.

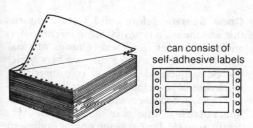

can consist of
self-adhesive labels

Control Character A character which when transmitted starts or controls a device. For example: a computer output having a particular **character** at the beginning may be routed to a **printer**, whereas with a different control character at the front it might be displayed on a **visual display unit**.

Control Register A **register** whose function is to hold the address of either the current **instruction** or the next instruction that the computer has to carry out.

Control Unit This is the part of the **central processing unit** which makes the computer carry out, in turn, each **instruction** of a program.

Core Store Before **solid state** memories this was the main type of store in all computers and consisted of rows and columns of small iron rings. They are like tiny washers which can be magnetised in one of two directions, clockwise or anticlockwise, thus giving **binary** storage. Still used widely today as they are non-**volatile**. Note that the cores are very small, even the largest being only a millimetre

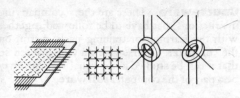

in diameter. When threaded with four wires through each (two read and two write) they look like tiny rows of soldiers, each row leaning in a different direction to the one before. They are built in sets of 32 × 32 giving 1024 (=1K) **bits** of **memory**.

Counter A name given to any device which continues to record 'the number of times' something is done. It might record the number of computer cards that are punched or, in the case of a program, the number of times a certain **loop** is carried out, though in the latter case the counter would be no more than a particular memory **location** whose value is increased by one each time.

For example: in a program when the computer expects, say, a 6-digit number, a counter could be used so that it waits for 6 digits but will accept no more.

45

Courseware These are the accompanying instructions that have to be followed together with the learning or training package run on the computer. Courseware may be printed so that it can be studied in the usual way but may be a part of the computer **software**.

Cray Seymour Cray. The designer of many of the most powerful computers in the world.

Critical Path This is a method of breaking down a large project into a series of ordered sequences. Each stage is then dependent on those before and predictions about time-scales can be made. Though not necessarily associated with computers, the method of critical path analysis usually involves a large amount of calculation best done by a computer.

Cross Compiler A **compiler** used by one computer to produce a **machine code** program suitable for another, usually smaller, computer.

Cursor Generally a rectangle the size of a capital letter which appears (sometimes flashing) on the screen of a **VDU** to indicate the current display position. Pressing a key should result in that **character** appearing on the screen in place of the cursor which is then displaced one character to the right.

Cybernetics The study of computer control in comparison with the human nervous system.

Daisy Wheel Printer This printer, as its name suggests, has a wheel with arms like the petals on a daisy. At the end of each arm there are two letters and these can be pressed forward by a hammer to print (about 50 characters per second) on paper using a typewriter ribbon.

10 characters per inch	12 characters per inch

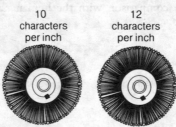

Data A general term for numbers, digits, characters and symbols which are accepted, stored and processed by a computer. Only when such data becomes meaningful to a person can we say we have '**information**'. Thus terms such as 'information processing' and '**information retrieval**' are really '**data processing**' and 'data retrieval'.

Database Really just files of **data** stored in

48

a computer but arranged so that they can be accessed in many different ways. The idea is that the same data is stored only once but is shared by various pieces of software.

For example: a database might contain three files; one on names of firms, one on addresses and one on types of business. Access to all three files for a particular company might be made using the company's name or by using the company's address.

Datalogging A term used to describe the automatic collecting of **data** by a machine for a computer, the data being stored for analysis at a later time.

For example: a **microprocessor** controlled central heating system would repeatedly record data from the heat sensors in the different rooms around the building. This data could be kept just as one might keep a log of one's journey though it would probably be used to control the heating.

Data processing Is the operation of collecting, storing, processing and transmitting **data**. A computer could be described as a data processing machine though a data processing system could involve clerical work and additional **hardware**.

Debugging A computer program may contain errors and these have to be found and corrected. As these errors are referred to as 'bugs' correcting them is known as debugging. The two main types of error are **logic** errors (the program subtracts B from A instead of A from B) and **syntax** errors (the instruction PRINT has been coded or typed in as PRNT).

Decimal An integer in the range 0 to 9 used in **denary notation**. Note that when working in denary (base 10) one uses the digits 0 to 1-less-than 10. Similarly when working in a different base, say 6, one uses the digits 0 to 1-less-than 6, that is 5. In binary (base 2) we just use 0 and 1.

Decision Box A symbol used in a **flowchart** to indicate a choice in direction. The choice is usually dependent upon the value of a **variable**.
For example:

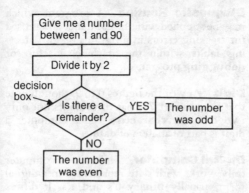

Decoder This is used to change **data** from one coded form into another.

For example: an instruction in a program such as PRINT would be stored in **binary** and as such would have to be decoded by **logic circuits** before it could be carried out.

Denary Notation Our normal number system where we count in tens using **decimals**. The digits 0 to 9 are used in the units column before we carry over to the tens column.

Diagnostic Routine A program which may be supplied with the computer and is used for tracking errors in programs or for detecting faults within the machine. Useful for **debugging** programs.

Digit Any of the figures 0 to 9, though note that the number 747 has three digits but only two different **characters**. To a computer a digit is part of an item of **data**.

Digital Computer This type of computer only works with **data** represented in a digital form, usually **binary** 0's and 1's. It differs from the **analogue computer** in that it can store large amounts of data and can calculate very accurately.

Digitiser This is a device which converts analogue signals into **digits**; that is an **A to D converter** (analogue to digital).

For example: in order that a computer might record readings of temperature one would connect the recording device to a computer via a digitiser. As the temperature rises so there would be a continuously increasing voltage input to the digitiser which is repeatedly scanned by the computer. The computer records the increases in finite jumps, storing the **data** as **digits**. Although the jumps can be made very small (thus giving greater accuracy and more significant figures) they always exist in the computer data.

Direct Access Memory Unlike **serial access**, direct access memory can be reached very quickly and without any reference to previous accessed locations. Sometimes called **random access memory** (RAM) the programmer can write into or read from any **address** without reading any other **data** first. For example: magnetic **disk** or **core store**.

Disk (or disc) A flat circular plate covered in magnetic material which is able to store data on its concentric tracks. As the disk spins a read/write head travels from edge to middle selecting only the required tracks. Each track is divided into **sectors**. Disks have fast access times (compared with tapes) and provide a popular non-**volatile** memory.

Disk Unit A peripheral device consisting of a disk drive and one or more read/write units.

Generally the disks themselves are removable from the disk unit. When inside the disks are accessed by the read/write head as they revolve at high speed.

Documentation This usually accompanies a computer program and gives advice on how to use the package and what output can be expected. It may also include a flowchart, a program listing, a list of **variables** and testing procedures with sample **data**. Documentation is useful to the program user but is vital if modifications are to be made to the program.

Document Reader An input device for a computer whereby forms having marks in certain positions are read (can be at high speed) by a machine.
For example: a sheet of questions having YES/NO boxes can be completed by many people, their responses being quickly analysed by a computer at a later time.

Double Buffering The use of two **buffers** in a computer where one can be analysed whilst the other is being filled and vice versa.

54

Double Length Word A facility of some microcomputers where two **words** can be operated as one double length word. This enables a computer having 8-**bit** words to be used as a 16-bit word machine.

Downloading Used to describe the taking of **data** from a large machine (**mainframe**) to a smaller one (**microcomputer**). This process might use the telephone, the radio or the television to provide the link between the two.

Down Time The length of time during which a machine is not usable due to faults of some kind.

Drum A cylindrical device coated on the outside with magnetic material which is able to store **data**. One or more read/write heads move along the side of the spinning drum selecting the required track.

Dump A word used to describe the process of copying the **data** in a section of memory and sending it to a peripheral device (a printer, say) or to a **backing store**.

Duplex Operation A mode of transmission which allows **data** to travel in both directions at the same time. It also displays on the screen the **character** typed as well as sending it to the computer. Half-duplex allows travel in both directions but not at the same time.

Dynamic Stop When running a program it may be necessary to draw the operator's attention to some factor or other. A dynamic stop jumps the program into an infinite **loop** at the same time indicating an **error** condition. Only after interaction by the operator will the machine resume processing.

Echo This is used as a check when transmitting **data**. What is received is returned to the original point and compared with the original data. If they are the same then the transmission has been carried out correctly.

Edge Connector

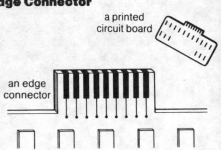

a printed circuit board

an edge connector

Where the conducting paths on a **printed circuit board** are taken to the edge to form a connector. Most boards have several edge connectors allowing the board to be plugged into a socket.

Edit The task of changing and improving a program by adding or removing instructions or by modifying the **data**. Sometimes done with the help of a special program called an 'editor'.

Eighty-Column Card Punched cards vary in shape and size according to the design of the computer for which they are used. However the most common are oblong in shape and have eighty columns, each column having twelve punched-hole positions.

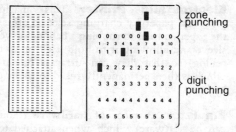

Electronic Device A device whose operation depends mainly on the behaviour of tiny charged particles called electrons. If used to store **data** it would be known as an electronic **memory**.

Electronic Mail A system where **data** is sent from one place to another via a **telecom-**

munications link. A letter typed on a word processor could be changed or corrected and then sent via a satellite communications system from an office in one country to a **VDU** screen in another country. Here it could be held in **memory** until required and then answered in the same way: no paper, no stamp, no postman; just an 'electronic office'.

Electrostatic Printer This machine prints on paper by charging selected areas of the paper (similar to rubbing a balloon on your sleeve and allowing it to hold itself on to the ceiling) so that they can attract a fine dust which is then permanently fused to the paper by heat.

Emulator A piece of **hardware** (though can be software) which when attached to a computer makes it behave as if it was another type of computer. Thus programs prepared for one range of computers can, with the aid of an emulator, be run on another range of computers.

Encoder A device (such as a keyboard or position indicator on a turning shaft) which converts signals into the coded digital form required for the next process.

End Mark   When working with a stream of **data** it is sometimes necessary to indicate the end of various items and this is done by using a particular code known as an end mark.

Epitaxy   A method of forming a thin layer of material (i.e. a **wafer**) on a base allowing materials other than **silicon** to be used for making **chips**.
For example: **gallium arsenide** wafers can be produced by firing ions of the material on to a base. When the wafer is formed the base is removed.

Erasable Storage   A storage medium which can be used over and over again as new **data** overwrites the old data.
For example: magnetic tape or magnetic disk.

Erase   The rubbing out of **data** that has been stored. However, unlike the rubbing out of a pencil line where nothing is left, in a computer it means replacing a code with another code that represents null data. It might be zeros but this is not necessarily the case. Each time data is stored, whether it is in the computer's memory or on disk or tape, this new data overwrites or erases what was originally stored.

Error This is said to have happened whenever the results that are expected do not appear. Errors can be due to mistakes made in programming (**software** errors) or due to faulty equipment (**hardware** errors).

Error Message When an error occurs it may be possible for the program to indicate what has gone wrong by putting a message on the screen. Such wording is known as an error message and helps the user find the fault quickly.

For example: 'cannot divide by zero at line 230' is an error message which tells the operator that the value of the denominator is zero at instruction number 230 in the program.

Exclusive-OR Gate This is a **logic gate** which operates with binary digits. Its output is of logic value 1 when any of its inputs have logic value 1 but not if all the inputs are 1.

(**Inclusive-OR** also outputs a 1 if all the inputs are 1).

For example: with a two input exclusive-OR the following **truth table** applies

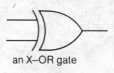

an X–OR gate

Input		Output
0	0	0
0	1	1
1	0	1
1	1	0

This gate could be used to sum two binary digits but does not give the carry digit.

Execute A word used to describe the carrying out of a program or of just a single instruction.

Exit This would result from the last instruction in a **routine** which would send the computer back to the main program; or it could be the ending of the whole program.

Extended BASIC BASIC is a computer programming language. Extended Basic would be a version which provides additional functions and facilities.

Facsimile The scanning of a document and converting the shading into electrical signals which can be transmitted via wires or radio waves. These signals are used to create a copy of the original document.

Fail Safe This term is used to describe a computer system or **peripheral** device which is able correctly to stop itself working should a fault occur.

Fast Line Rates of transmitting **data** are usually given in **baud**. **Prestel** transmits to the user at 1200 baud although data at this speed on telephone lines can get lost or muddled. Special direct lines, available from British Telecom, are able to transmit data at 48000 or 96000 baud. Such lines would be known as fast lines.

Feasibility Study This is carried out before a company buys a new computer system. A team of experts (**system analysts**) would study the problem to see whether a computer was necessary and what sort of machine would best suit the company.

Ferrite Core A ring-shaped piece of magnetic material the size of a pin-head or smaller. Just as a bar of iron can be magnetised N–S or S–N so a ring can be magnetised clockwise or anticlockwise, and this is used for storing binary 0's and 1's. Such cores are built in rows to form what is known as the **core store** of a computer.

Fibre Optics Concerned with the transmission of light along a glass or Perspex fibre. Light entering one end of a fibre is repeatedly reflected on the outside of the inner part until it reaches the other end. Total internal reflection takes place as two types of glass are used and this involves very little energy being lost at each reflection.

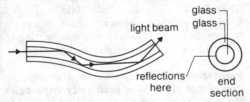

Such fibres are made very thin (less than 1 mm across) and are easily bent. Thus a cable consisting of many fibres can be laid in just the same way as normal copper ones, though many more signals can be carried for the same size cable. Normal electrical signals (carrying data) are used to modulate a laser light beam which is sent to a receiver by an optical fibre.

Field Effect Transistor (FET) As opposed to the bipolar or **junction transistor** this **semiconductor** device works by regulating the current as it flows through a narrow channel. FETs, as they are often called, are both smaller and cheaper than bipolar transistors. In terms of logic **gates** on a silicon chip the greater densities are achieved with FETs.

File Just as sheets of paper form a file in a filing cabinet so a collection of **data** can form a file in a computer **memory**. Each computer file would have its own file name consisting of a limited set (say six or eight) of **characters**.

Firmware A word used to describe programs that are held in **read only memories** (ROM). These can be accessed very quickly and are not lost when the machine is switched off (non-**volatile** memory). Thus they do not have to be loaded into the computer as they are permanently available in the machine.

First Generation Computers These computers, built in the 1940's and early 50's, used electronic valves, whereas the **second generation**, built between the mid 50's and the mid 60's, used transistors. The **third generation** used integrated circuits.

Fixed Disk Store Although the disk rotates it is not possible with this type to remove or change the disk. However far greater storage capacities are available.

Fixed Point Arithmetic This system involves having the decimal point of every number in the correct place, though the position can be set before a calculation (i.e. all figures to two decimal places). This does limit the size of numbers though permits faster calculations by the computer.

Flag An indicator added to the end of a piece of **data** which might be used to indicate an error or to make the **hardware** perform a branch to another part of the program.

Flat-Bed Plotter A piece of equipment controlled by a computer that draws lines on paper. The pen can be moved in two directions independently and can be lifted. For colour drawings several coloured pens are used, one being selected at a time.

Flip-Flop A basic electronic circuit which remains in one of two possible states until it receives a signal. It then switches over to the other state and waits for the next signal before switching back. Known technically as a **bi-stable** multivibrator it can be used as a storage device (two states, one for 0 and one for 1) or for division by two as two input pulses are required to get it to give out one pulse.

Floating Point Arithmetic Unlike **fixed point**, these numbers are recorded as a set of digits together with the power to which their base is raised.

For example: the denary number 789.249 would be stored as (+0789249) and (+3). Most scientific calculators use this method which, although slower in calculations, gives a very much wider range of numbers. Note the convention of using E so that the number can be written as 0.789249E3 and that the EE key converts this to 7.89249E2.

Floppy Disk A flexible magnetic disk used for supplying and storing **data** for a **microcomputer**. When the disk rotates inside its cardboard jacket (say 300 r.p.m.) in a **disk unit** it becomes rigid and can be 'read' by the read/write head. The area used for recording is a band of concentric tracks each of which is divided into **sectors**. Disks may be single or double sided, single or double density and soft or hard sectored. They are available in three sizes, $3\frac{1}{2}$ inch, $5\frac{1}{4}$ inch (**mini-floppy**) and 8 inch diameters and hold on one side about 50, 100 and 300 kilo**bytes** respectively (normal density).

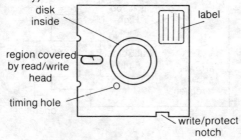

Flowchart A set of special boxes or shapes drawn on paper and connected by lines to show the order of a set of events. Used by programmers to describe the sequence of operations to be carried out by a computer.
For example: adjusting the pressure of a tyre.

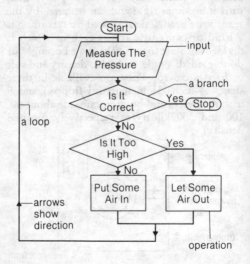

Format As one would expect this is the setting down of the layout to be used. In computing terms formatting usually refers to the initialising of a new **floppy disk**, or the arranging of the layout of a piece of text prior to its being printed.

FORTRAN (acronym for **FOR**mula **TRAN**slation) This **high level language** was designed in the early 1950's as a scientific problem-solving language.

Frame An often misunderstood word in that it describes one screenful (about 150 words if all text) of information on the **Prestel** system. Prestel pages can consist of one or more frames. It is also used to describe one row of holes across a **paper tape** (which is the code for a single **character**) and one **bit** of store across a magnetic tape (a 0 or 1).

Function Code A computer instruction has two parts. The function or operation code states what has to be done (add, subtract, print) and the other part indicates on what (numbers, address).

Gallium Arsenide A **semiconductor** that is used instead of silicon when high speed circuits are required on a **chip**. The other advantage is that they require less power though they are at present much more expensive to make. Gallium arsenide **wafers** are usually made by ion beam **epitaxy** and one process involves production on the American space shuttle.

Garbage The name given to meaningless **data**. Such rubbish is printed by a computer because of errors in the program or in the data or because the data belongs to another program. 'Garbage in–garbage out' (GIGO) is a well-known saying with regard to computers.

Gate Electronically this word refers to a part of the **field effect transistor** though it is generally used to describe a **logic circuit** with several inputs and one or two outputs.
For example: an **AND gate** where the output depends on the logic state of the inputs. Such gates form the basic building units of all calculating chips.

Germanium A **semiconductor** which was used a great deal in the 1950's for making transistors and other devices. Largely replaced by **silicon** in the 60's.

Grandfather With **data** that is **updated** on occasions it is normal to keep the last two versions as a safeguard. The three versions kept separately are known as 'grandfather', 'father' and 'son'.

Graphical Display Such a unit, rather like the screen of a television set, is used to display both text and drawings. Sometimes a **light pen** can be used by the operator to get the computer to make changes to the display.

Graph Plotter An output device which enables the computer to draw graphs and pictures. Sometimes a pen moves in two directions above a flat piece of paper (**X–Y Plotter**). There can be more than one pen, say four or more, each of a different colour.

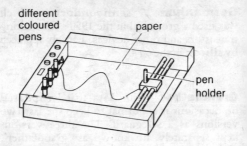

Other devices allow the paper holder to move back and forth in one direction and the pen to move at right angles. A drum plotter has the paper fixed to a drum which rotates back and forth.

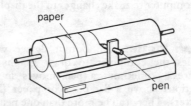

Half-Adder A logic circuit (which consists of a set of **gates**) which has two inputs and two outputs. It is used to add together two **binary digits** giving both the sum and the carry digit.

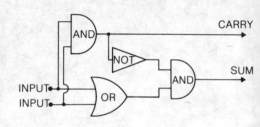

Handpunch A mechanical device for punching holes. In the case of **punched cards**, on punching one (or two) of the twelve buttons the corresponding holes are punched and the card moves forward one column. In the case of **paper tape** the operator generally has a full keyboard, the tape moving forward after each character is punched.

Handshake This is an extra signal that is transmitted along a separate wire when **data** is transferred from one machine to another. It in fact controls the transfer by indicating the different **blocks** as they are sent. Not all machines accept a handshake line.

Hard copy This is the printed output, usually on paper, which can be taken away and studied.

Hard Sectored This describes the way in which the length of a **sector** on a **floppy disk** is set. In this case small holes (say 6 or 12 in a ring) near the centre hole of the disk fix the length of each sector: as the disk revolves they indicate the change from one to the next.

Hardware This is the name given to all the equipment that makes up the computer system. If it can be picked up and carried then it is hardware as opposed to **software**.

Hardwired Logic This is the logic that is built-in to a **chip** by the manufacturer and refers to the wiring between **gates** as well as the gates themselves.

Hash Total In a file the computer adds together a reference digit or number from each item thus giving a meaningless total or hash total. This is used on future occasions to check that all the items have been accessed.

Heuristic Program A program so written that each time it solves a problem it learns from itself and makes changes to improve its performance the next time.

Hexadecimal Notation In this system one counts in 'sixteens' instead of 'tens'. Usually the **digits** 0 to 9 are used and the letters A, B, C, D, E and F represent ten, eleven, twelve, thirteen, fourteen and fifteen. Whereas in a four-digit number in denary each digit in turn represents thousands, hundreds, tens and units, in HEX each digit would represent 4096's, 256's, 16's and units.
Thus

$$A60B = (10 \times 4096) + (6 \times 256) + (0 \times 16) + (11 \times 1)$$
$$= 42507 \text{ in denary}$$

The reason for HEX being used by computers is because of the way numbers are stored. To store the numbers 0 to 9 in binary, four digits are required, 0000 to 0101. Thus for our normal numbers we have to use four binary digits, but with four binary digits we can store not just 0 to 9, but 0 to 15. That is 0000 to 1111. So by working in sixteens we can use all the available storage codes that the computer can offer.

High Level Language A programming language in which each instruction corresponds to several **machine code** instructions, and is easy for the user to understand. Before running, the high level program might be compiled into machine code or each instruction may be interpreted in turn. FORTRAN, COBOL and BASIC are all examples of high level languages and most machine manufacturers would, for example, offer both a BASIC **compiler** and a BASIC **interpreter**.

High Resolution Graphics Most **microcomputers** offer some form of graphics whereby the programmer is able to plot points and draw lines. Whether a diagonal line across the screen looks straight or like a set of steps depends upon the size of each point plotted which in turn depends on the total number of points across and up-and-down. As a rough guide 150 by 100 points on a screen would be low resolution whilst 600 by 250 would be considered high.

Hollerith Herman Hollerith (USA 1860–1929). He realised that the results of the 1890 United States census would not be worked out by hand before the 1900 census was due and so devised a card-reading machine to analyse the census details. The punched card code he invented allowed all twenty-six letters and the numbers 0 to 9 to be coded in twelve punching positions. Known as the Hollerith Code, it is still in use today.

Hopper A device that holds punched cards ready for feeding to a **card punch** or **card reader**.

Housekeeping These are routines, sometimes within a program, that are carried out when time is not of importance.

For example: the setting up of suitable fields or entry conditions or the allocation of areas of store or the updating of the master record-keeping file.

Hybrid Computer This is a computer in which analogue and digital devices are interconnected so that **data** can be transferred between them. Usually found in science laboratories or as the controlling device in an industrial process.

Identifier A name or set of **characters** chosen by the programmer which indicates which **file** or which store is to be used at that point in the program.

Immediate Access Store This is used to describe those **memories** where **data** can be accessed in times of one millionth of a second (a microsecond) or less. Included would be those stores within the **central processor** and those directly addressable by the programmer.

Inclusive-OR Gate This is a **logic gate** which operates with **binary digits**. Its output is of logic value 1 when any of its inputs has a logic value 1, otherwise it is 0.

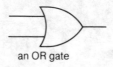

an OR gate

For example: with a two input inclusive-OR gate the following **truth table** applies.

Input		Output
0	0	0
0	1	1
1	0	1
1	1	1

Incremental Plotter As opposed to an **X–Y plotter** which requires X and Y values, this unit plots or draws according to **data** supplied by the computer which moves it from its current position. Each plot is therefore relative to the previous plot and not to a fixed origin.

Indexed Sequential Access This is the storing and retrieving of **data** from a sequence of stores whose addresses have to be first found by the computer from an index file.

Indirect Addressing This is where the address in one program instruction refers to another location which contains another address. Used by programmers to access a series of addresses with just one instruction whose address is increased by one each time it is carried out.

For example: a programming instruction might say 'Recall the number stored in the location whose address is given in store XXX'. Store XXX is then increased by one each time.

Information What is obtained from **data** by humans when they apply a set of rules.
For example: the data on this page is conveying information to the reader (the author hopes) because a set of rules (i.e. English words and sentences) are being applied by the reader. Note that a computer really only deals with data.

Information Retrieval A part of computing technology that allows speedy access to part of a **database**. In the past 'finding out' took time, allowing the user to think and plan. With today's on line databases one has to plan the search route before starting, as pages of information appear so quickly.

Initialise The setting up of the values of the variables at the start of a program so as to

clear the values set by the previous run.
For example: **counters** would be set to zero or their initial values.

Ink-Jet Printer   Here a fine jet of quick-drying ink is fired at the paper forming characters as it lands. The ink droplets become charged as they are fired through the jet and can then be bent into shape by a varying electric field. Speeds as high as 200 characters per second can be achieved and the device has the advantage of not being limited by the number of metal characters that can be positioned for printing. In addition, character sets and type styles can be controlled by the program and many different languages can be printed with the same printer.

Input Device   This is the device which is between the human being and the machine and enables both program and **data** to enter the computer.
For example: **punched cards** or **punched tape**. Also **light pen**, **keyboard**, **bar code** reader and **optical** or **mark sense** reader.

Instruction This is part of a computer program and it is the part that tells the computer what it should be doing at that stage. For example: PRINT or ADD.

Instruction Address Register (IAR) This **register** stores in turn the **addresses** of the instructions that the computer has to carry out. If during a program you could look inside this register you would find that it contained the address of the next instruction.

Insulator A material that has a very high resistance to electric current so that the current flow through it is negligible. One of the best insulators known is silicon dioxide which is created on the surface of silicon by heating.

Integrated Circuit (IC) or Chip A **solid state** circuit in which all the components are formed upon a single piece of **semiconductor** material. The first one consisted of a transistor and a resistor and was created in 1959. Since then the number of components on a 'chip' has nearly doubled each year. LSI (large scale integration) means an integrated circuit with more than 100 **logic gates** or over 1000 memory **bits**.

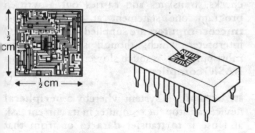

Intelligent Terminal A terminal which retains a program and allows processing of **data** to be carried out without further access to the computer.

Interface This is the circuitry (or **hardware**) needed between two devices so that they can be connected together. Such a circuit board might compensate for differences in speed-of-working or transmission speeds or might translate the codes. Often it is the type of transmission that has to be changed and the interface is attached inside one of the devices.

Interpreter A type of program which checks, translates and carries out a written program one statement at a time. Most **microcomputers** are supplied with a **BASIC** interpreter which, though satisfactory for most purposes, is much slower running than a BASIC **compiler**.

Interrupt A system whereby a **peripheral** device can stop the computer in its current task and use it to transfer **data** to or from that peripheral. The computer would then return to continue its work.

Inverted File A method of organising a file so that groups are identified by 'keys'. Thus retrieving various groups is much quicker than by the normal method of searching every record. As **information retrieval** becomes widely used so file inversion becomes more important.

Iteration This is a mathematical process by which one obtains an answer and then uses that answer to obtain a more accurate one. The new answer is then used to obtain an even better one and so on. Whereas with pencil and paper such a method would be long and slow, with a computer it is a very useful way of finding the best answer.

Jack Plug   A type of plug that offers quick and easy connection in that its single pin is pushed into a socket as far as it will go. Used by British Telecom for both movable telephones (4-way) and **Prestel** receivers (5-way) and thus are used to connect microcomputers (British Telecom approved) to the telecommunications network.

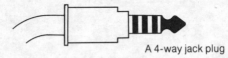

A 4-way jack plug

These are now being superseded by a smaller horizontal 6-way strip connecting plug.

Jacquard   Joseph Jacquard (France 1752–1834). He used punched cards to store machine operating instructions. His automatic weaving loom was controlled by the punched holes in cards.

Job Control Language (JCL)   A set of commands designed for a particular computer which are used to run a program. Such commands may involve loading a **compiler**, reading in the program, allocating memory and processing time and limiting the printer output. The same set of commands may be used regularly and in such case would be stored as a job control file.

Josephson Memory The ultimate magnetic memory device which will operate at up to a hundred times faster than today's best **chips** with even greater reductions in power consumption. These memory cells are kept at very low temperatures using liquid helium. With several problems still to be solved Josephson memories are not likely to be readily available until the 1990's.

Joy Stick Like the paddles this is another input device for a microcomputer. The stick as it moves is able to control the movement of a shape on the screen. It does this by working two potentiometers (like the volume control on a radio), one recording its movement in the X-direction and the other in the Y-direction. Often there are two joy sticks enabling a screen game to be played by two players.

Junction Transistor This is sometimes called the bipolar transistor or just 'transistor'.

As opposed to the **field effect transistor** (FET) this **semiconductor** device works by regulating the current across a junction or boundary between **p-type** and **n-type** materials. Their advantage over FET's is that they are faster acting.

Justify   This is the adjustment of the positions of words so that the left-hand or right-hand margins or both, are regular. This is easily done on **text** by a computer before the words are printed.

For example: the paragraph above is both left- and right-hand justified whilst this paragraph is only left-hand justified the lines being different lengths.

Keyboard This is a device for coding **characters** on to **punched cards**, **punched tape** or directly into a computer. In addition to the standard typewriter (QWERTY) pattern there are numeric keys, user definable keys, **hexadecimal** keys and others.

For example: the **microwriter** keys.

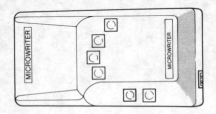

Key-to-Disk Unit A stand-alone device that allows **data** from a **keyboard** to be put directly on to **disk**.

Keyword Often used in **information retrieval** systems whereby items containing the given keyword are accessed by the computer and retrieved. In simpler systems only the titles of the stored items may be searched for the particular keyword though with some **mainframe** computers every word in the **database** can be checked.

Kilo- (K)   This prefix generally signifies 'one thousand' as for example in a rate of transmission of **data**. 96 kilo**baud** means 96000 **bits** per second. However in terms of computer storage 1K is 1024 (which is 2 to the power of 10) and so 16K of memory means 16384 **bytes**.

Kimball Tag   Small pieces of card with holes usually attached to goods in a shop and removed at the time of purchase. These are used as **punched card** input for a computer which is thereby able to keep sales records and provide management reports.

Instead of holes the data is sometimes coded in a magnetic strip on the tag.

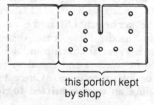

this portion kept
by shop

Language In order to tell a computer what to do we have to use a language it understands. In addition the language we use must be precise with no chance of a double meaning. Such languages have been developed over the years from **machine code** and mnemonics to **high level languages** like **BASIC** and **PASCAL**.

Language Symbolique d'Enseignement (LSE) A **high level language** developed in the early 1970's in France for use in education.

Large Scale Integration (LSI) This is a measure of the number of **logic gates** on a chip. **Small scale integration** (SSI) about 1961, has less than 20; **medium scale integration** (MSI) about 1965, between 20 and 100; and large scale integration about 1969, above 100. Today we have VLSI (above 5000) though the **acronym** LSI is the one that is commonly used. Note that the **microprocessor** is a special LSI chip and that the LSI chips used in watches and calculators are unlikely to be microprocessors. Current practice is to produce an **uncommitted logic array**

(ULA) chip which can have its logic gates connected in different ways for different customers. This is a cheaper and quicker way of obtaining a special type of chip as only one stage of manufacture is particular to that customer. However the design is limited by the original logic gates and the possible connections between them.

Least Significant Character In a set or row of characters the one in the furthest right-hand position is the least significant one.

Left Justification This as opposed to **right justification** is the arranging of lines of text so that the left-hand edges are all in line. However it can also refer to **data** stored in consecutive locations all of which have been filled from the left though they may have a different number of spaces on the right.

Leibniz Gottfried Leibniz (German 1646–1716). He designed in about 1670 a machine which could multiply and divide as well as add and subtract like **Pascal's** machine. This was the forerunner of the desk-top mechanical calculating machine.

Library Software These are the programs and routines available to all the users of a particular computer. They form part of the facilities of the computer.

Light Emitting Diode (LED) A small coloured device that emits light like a bulb. It is particularly useful as an indicator lamp in such things as computers, television sets and radios as it requires a very low current and works at low voltages. Used in the past in calculators and digital wrist-watches but largely replaced by **liquid crystal displays** (LCD) which require even less power.

Light Guide The name given to glass or Perspex fibre used to transfer optical signals. Light enters at one end and is totally internally reflected along the **fibre optic** – that is guided by the fibre.

Light Pen Used with a graphical display unit the light pen allows the operator to draw, change and move sections of the picture simply by moving the pen across the screen. The pen is connected by cable to the computer and the operator uses keys to control the

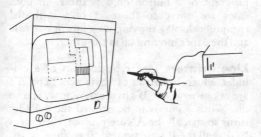

changes. A television picture is produced by a dot which moves across the screen in lines (625) and the position of the pen can be worked out by the computer from the timings of the dot as it passes. Although the original programming for a light pen is complicated its use can enable designs to be created and changed very quickly.

For example: certain shapes can be stored in the computer's memory and then created on the screen in positions set by the pen just by pressing a key.

Line Feed   This can be an instruction in a program or a button on a **printer**. In both cases we move to the next line, with the computer display moving up a line in one case and the paper moving up in the other.

Line Printer   One type consists of a cylinder which has rows of characters. The A's are in one row, the B's in the next row, and so on. When a line is to be printed the cylinder turns so that all the A's are printed, then turns so that all the B's are printed, then the C's; the whole line being printed in one revolution of the cylinder. Printing speed is between 500 and 3000 lines per minute but the lines printed are usually wavy.

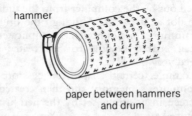

hammer

paper between hammers
and drum

For example: the line printer would print COLLINS COMPUTER GEM on one line by printing like this:

```
C         C              E
C         C          E  GE
C         C          E  GE
C   I     C          E  GE
C LLI     C          E  GE
C LLI     C M        E  GEM
C LLIN    C M        E  GEM
COLLIN    COM        E  GEM
COLLIN    COMP       E  GEM
COLLIN    COMP    ER GEM
COLLINS   COMP    ER GEM
COLLINS   COMP TER GEM
COLLINS   COMPUTER   GEM
```

Liquid Crystal Display (LCD) Consists of a liquid whose molecules can be made to line up thus making it look darker when an electrical voltage is applied. Used in **seven segment displays** on watches and **calculators** as they require little power. Some liquid crystals change in colour with temperature and can be used as crude thermometers.

List Generally referred to as the listing on screen or paper of the program statements in number order. To follow the program statements in execution order one would use a **trace** facility.

Load The reading of program statements or **data** from **backing store** into the appropriate parts of the computer **memory**.

Location The name given to the places in a computer that are able to store **data**. Each location is identified and accessed by its **address** and the number of characters that can be stored in a location depends upon the particular machine.

Logic Circuit The basic building blocks of digital electronics often referred to as **Logic Gates**. **AND**, **OR**, **NAND** and **NOR** are all examples of logic circuits and it is these that make up the circuits on a silicon chip. In an **uncommitted logic array** (ULA) chip sets of logic circuits await interconnection to achieve the required circuit pattern.

Log In/On/Off/Out Is the term used when entering or leaving a large computer system from a **terminal**. In this way the number of users can be limited and the type of use restricted.

Look-Up Table The dialling-codes of all the towns and cities in the United Kingdom could be stored in a **table** in the **memory** of a computer. By typing in the place name, say Cambridge, the computer would use a 'look-up table' to find the correct dialling-code which would be 0223 in this case. Such a table would be arranged as an **array**.

Loop Just as a loop of thread comes back to where it started so does a loop in a computer program. One difference is that the program continues to loop back until a certain condition is satisfied.

For example: the sorting of a set of numbers into ascending order would involve the computer in carrying out a sequence of instructions over and over again (a loop) until all the numbers were sorted. One way is to:

COMPARE THE FIRST AND SECOND NUMBERS

IF FIRST IS GREATER, INTERCHANGE NUMBERS
NOW REPEAT THIS LOOP WITH SECOND AND THIRD NUMBERS and so on. When all the numbers have been dealt with REPEAT LOOP starting with first and second numbers again. A run through of all the numbers without any changes means that they are in order. Note that a loop inside another loop is called a nested loop.

Low Level Language   The name given to a computer **language** which is similar to and easily converted into **machine code**. Each **instruction** is converted into one machine code instruction and is executed by the computer as a single operation. It is used when speed is of importance. With a **high level language** (such as **BASIC** or **FORTRAN**) one instruction would involve many machine code operations on the part of the computer.

Lyons Electronic Office (LEO)   One of the first commercial computers built in 1953 by the teashop company J. Lyons & Co. and used in the first instance to calculate staff wages.

Machine Code This is the coding that makes the computer carry out its various tasks. The types of instruction and the way they have to be written are specified by the computer manufacturer. Machine code programming has often to be done in **binary notation** and is used when fast operation is required.

For example: **instruction** number 634 might be to subtract (code 2) the contents of **location** 102 from the contents of 101 and put the answer in location 103. This might be machine coded as:

$$634 \quad 2 \quad 101 \quad 102 \quad 103$$

It should be clear that programming in machine code is slow and tedious. The programmer has to keep track of what is held in each location and specify these locations in each instruction. To make things easier manufacturers supply an assembly language or **assembler** which uses words and letters to represent operations and **addresses**.

SUB A,B,C

would mean subtract the value of B from the value of A and let C be the value of the answer.

The assembler translates each instruction into one machine code instruction. For easier programming a **high level language** such as **BASIC** is used and the instruction becomes:

$$LET \ C = A - B$$

A **compiler** or **interpreter** would then be used to translate such an instruction into machine code, though many machine code instructions would be required for each high level language instruction.

Magnetic Ink This is used when printing characters on forms which can be automatically read or sorted by machine as well as by people. The characters are distinctive in that they are made up of thick and thin lines.

For example: the numbers along the bottom

of each bank cheque are printed in magnetic ink. On receipt of a completed cheque the bank staff type the amount on to the cheque itself in magnetic ink and using a magnetic ink **character** reader linked to a computer all the necessary calculations and deductions are carried out automatically.

Magnetic Memory Just as a bar of iron can be magnetised with a north pole at one end and a south at the other (or the other way round) so other magnetic materials can be magnetised in two ways. This is used to represent a 0 or a 1 and is thus able to store **characters** in **binary notation**. Magnetic **core store** consists of tiny iron-type washers half a millimetre in diameter wired in sets of 1024 (32 × 32) giving 1K of **memory**. Magnetic **tape** or card using several tracks can hold over 1000 **characters** per inch and transmit several inches worth to a computer per second. Magnetic **disks** may be hard (rigid) or floppy (flexible) and store characters on concentric tracks. Hard disks may be arranged in sets of say six, such a pack being removable from the **disk unit** or as a single disk in the case of a **winchester disk drive**. Whereas **floppy**

disks would hold a few hundred kilo**bytes**, hard disks hold several Megabytes (Mega = million).

Mainframe This term is used to describe the **central processing unit** (CPU) of a large computer which has many **terminals**. Originally the words referred to the framework used to hold the CPU and **arithmetic logic unit** (ALU).

Main Store This is the **memory** of the computer that can be accessed immediately. **Core store** and **solid state** memory are used for the main store whilst magnetic tape and disk are used as **backing store**.

Maintenance Contract Most computer manufacturers and computer repair companies offer service contracts on equipment. Such contracts may include preventive maintenance whereby the machine is serviced regularly in addition to guaranteed call-out times (i.e. the engineer will visit four times each year and within 24 hours of a fault being reported). Some maintenance contracts include labour charges but not the cost of replacement parts: a full service contract would include both.

Mark Sense Cards Computer cards (which may be punched cards) divided into columns allowing spaces for marking with a pencil line. (Mark sense forms are also available). These marks can then be read electrically by a machine (mark sense reader) linked to a computer or card punch. Similar to optical scanning where the marks are read by a light-sensor. Both methods are useful for collecting and analysing responses to multiple-choice type questions.

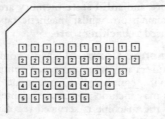

Matrix Printer A **printer** which forms characters on paper by printing a pattern of dots. The printing head consists of a set of horizontal needles mounted one above the other in a line. As the head moves sideways certain wires are pushed forward to form a column of dots on the paper and several such columns form a **character**. Early matrix heads had seven needles but were unable to print lower-case descenders (the tail of a g or y). Now nine needles are used but there are printers with sixteen, eighteen and even twenty-four needles. A range of colours can be achieved by using say a four-colour ribbon and over-printing in different colour(s).

For example: a nine-wire dot matrix printer uses five dots for a small letter plus two above for capitals and two below for lower-case descenders.

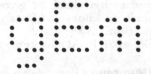

An improved print is obtained by printing each character twice particularly if the second print is slightly out of line with the first, making the gaps between the dots less obvious.

Medium Scale Integration (MSI) This is a measure of the number of **logic gates** on a single **chip**.

Small scale integration (SSI)	less than 20
Medium scale integration (MSI)	20 to 100
Large scale integration (LSI)	100 to 5000
Very large scale integration (VLSI)	over 5000

Mega- (M) A million.
For example:
$$1 \text{ Mbyte} = 1 \text{ Megabyte}$$
$$= 1000000 \text{ bytes}$$

Memory A computer's memory is made up of its **main store** and its **backing store**. Sizes are measured in **bytes** and are given as so many K meaning **kilo**bytes. (**Data** or program **instructions** may be stored).
For example: a 32K RAM microcomputer.

Memory Mapping Items of **data** are often more easily accessed if they are stored in an **array**. However the computer **memory** consists of **locations** one after the other, and data, though arranged in an array can be stored sequentially. The arranging or mapping of arrays in this way (in a 'known' part of the memory) takes less space than arrays created in a **high level language**. Memory mapping is also useful for sending data to **peripherals**, in particular to a visual display unit (VDU). Here data is made to appear on a peripheral device simply by putting it in a certain part of the **immediate access store**.

Memory Switching System As its name implies this communications system uses a computer to accept messages from its terminals, stores them if necessary and then transmits them to other terminals as indicated by the message.

Microcomputer A computer which uses a **microprocessor** chip such as the Motorola 6502, the Zilog Z80A or the Intel 8088 for its central processor.

Microelectronics That section of electronics which uses extremely small electronic parts. **Integrated circuits** are one example where cost, size, weight and power consumption have been reduced considerably coupled with an increase in reliability.

Microfiche The name given to a photographic-like slide (or film in the case of 'microfilm') which is viewed using a special type of projector. Pages of print, diagrams and graphs are considerably reduced in size and stored in this way. A 6×4 inch microfiche could hold up to 250 pages whereas a continuous roll of microfilm might hold 2000 pages. Computer **output** can be directly put on to microfiche or microfilm using a **cathode-ray tube** (CRT) picture (which is reduced in size) or a special laser printer. In addition to the size there is a considerable weight reduction compared with printed paper output. Using special machines it is possible for a computer to select and read pages from microfilm.

Microprocessor A special LSI **chip** that is used as the **central processing unit** of a computer. It is able to receive and store **data**, perform arithmetical and logic operations according to its stored program and give out the results. In addition to **microcomputers** their use is so wide that it is difficult to suggest an area in which they will not be used. Applications today include cookers and washing machines, cars and aircraft, machine tool control and remote monitoring of oil fields, video machines, bank cash dispensers and public telephone boxes.

Microwriter A portable gadget with a six-key **keyboard**, (designed to replace the traditional outdated **QWERTY** keyboard) a one-line display and a **memory**. By pressing different groups of keys different **characters** are put into memory. Used to write, store and edit letters and reports anywhere (say on a plane or train) which can if required be transferred to a word processor on return to the office.

Minicomputer The minicomputer is the name given to small-sized machines that, in comparison to **mainframe** computers, have limited **memory** and a few **peripheral** devices. Being between the fixed-position mainframe and the portable **microcomputer** in size (similar to a wardrobe) it is generally used to do one specific job.

Mini-Floppy At the present time this is the most popular form of **random access mem-**

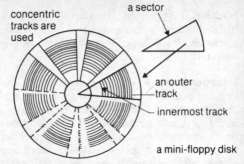

concentric tracks are used

a sector

an outer track

innermost track

a mini-floppy disk

ory for microcomputers. It consists of a 5¼ inch flexible magnetic disk inside a cardboard cover which has sections cut away for the disk drive unit (**disk unit**) and the read/write head to access the disk. When spinning at around 300 revs per minute the disk is rigid and the head moves in a straight line between the centre and the edge. Just as a cassette tape recorder uses parallel tracks on a tape so a disk drive uses concentric circular tracks on a disk. These circular tracks, around 40 in number each side, are divided into sectors and although the length of track in a sector is shorter near the middle of the disk it still takes the same time to pass the head. Thus data is more compact on the inner tracks of a disk.

118

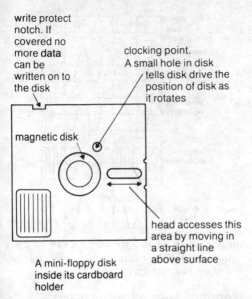

write protect notch. If covered no more **data** can be written on to the disk

clocking point. A small hole in disk tells disk drive the position of disk as it rotates

magnetic disk

head accesses this area by moving in a straight line above surface

A mini-floppy disk inside its cardboard holder

Modulation The technique of using **data** signals to modify a transmitted wave so that the wave carries the data signals. There are three ways in which a wave can be affected – by changing its amplitude (size) or its fre-

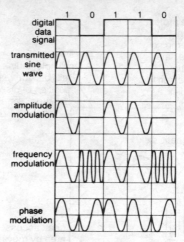

quency or its phase. By varying one of these using a MODEM a data signal can be superimposed on a carrier wave.

Monitor Most **microcomputers** will display their output on a television set, the signal being accepted via the aerial socket. For better definition, particularly with graphics, a monitor is required which accepts a **video** signal. This signal has a lower frequency though it can be either black and white or colour. In addition there are RGB monitors which accept separate signals for the three colours, red, green and blue, which make up the picture on a colour screen. The word monitor is also used to describe any device or a part of the operating system that examines what is happening in a computer system and takes action if something is wrong.

Most Significant Character   The **character** on the extreme left of a set of characters.

Mother Board   Some **microcomputers** consist of more than one **printed circuit board**. There may be a board to control access to the **disk** drives; one to provide **high resolution graphics**; one for colour; one to support the input/output user ports; and so on. The board that holds and supports all the other boards is known as the mother board. Sometimes this is also the board that holds the **microprocessor** and thus controls access to the other boards. However there are computers with only one board (single-board computers) and computers contained on a single chip (microcontroller).

Multi-Access System Such a system allows many users access to one computer. Airline seat reservation from many offices around the country is one example. Most multi-access systems give the user the impression that they alone are using the computer, though it is during the time they take to press the keys that the computer serves other users. All such systems rely on **time sharing**.

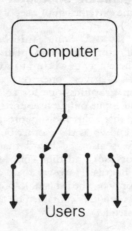

Computer

Users

Multiplexor A device which controls the transmission of **data** between a computer and its many users. The multiplexor is able to switch very quickly so that data along a single wire can be routed from or to many different wires each one behaving as if it had continuous contact. Often multiplexors are used in pairs some distance apart each having many connections though only one path exists between them. This might be of wire, glass fibre or microwaves.

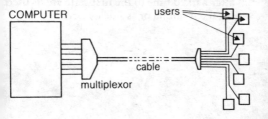

Multivibrator A basic electronic circuit that can be built using two transistors and a few components. There are three types:

The **astable** multivibrator which continuously switches from one of its two states to the other and is used in computers as a clock.

The **bistable** multivibrator which rests in one or other of its two states and is used to store a **binary digit**. Sometimes known as a '**flip-flop**'.

The monostable multivibrator which when switched to the other state always reverts after a fixed time to the first state and is used for fixed timing or as a delay circuit.

NAND Gate A logic gate the same as **NOT AND** (Not AND) whose **truth table** with two inputs would be:

Input		Output
0	0	1
0	1	1
1	0	1
1	1	0

a NAND gate

It is worth noting that by joining the two inputs together on a NAND gate it becomes a **NOT** gate or an inverter.

Input	Output
0	1
1	0

Napier John Napier (Scottish 1550–1617).
He invented a very simple device for doing
multiplication known as Napier's Rods. It
consisted of a set of eleven rods divided into
numbered sections which when put side by
side enabled multiplication by a single digit.
Thus to multiply 634 by 58 the results of
'times 50' and 'times 8' were added together.
However he is better remembered as the person who invented logarithms thus enabling
complicated multiplication and division to be
done easily. This invention led to slide rules
and simple calculating machines, the forerun-
ners of today's computers.

Negation The operation of changing
something into its opposite. The negation of
the binary number 101 would produce 010.
Each **binary digit** is changed to the opposite
one. 'Negation plus one' enables one to find
the **'two's complement'** of a binary number,
the advantage being that we can use the
normal rules of addition and subtraction with
negative numbers.
For example:

Number	Negation (1's complement)	Negation + 1 (2's complement)
0101	1010	1011
010100	101011	101100
0111	1000	1001
0110 (+6)	1001	1010 (−6)

The third column is the 'two's complement' of the first column. In a system of positive and negative binary numbers the leftmost **bit** is used to indicate the sign; 0 for positive, 1 for negative. However with a 1, only the first bit is negative (place values are −8, +4, +2 and +1) thus the last line of the table above tells us that −6 (from −8 + 2) is the two's complement of +6 (+4 + 2).

Network Networks allow **data** (which may be computer programs) to be sent over long distances between a set of computers. In a true network system each user is able to access all the facilities available on the system, the advantage being that they can all share the same **printer** and **backing store**.

Noise Noise is the cause of errors in **data** that has been transmitted via a telephone wire. Random changes in voltage, frequency or phase can cause a change in the signal being transmitted and this results in the wrong code arriving at the receiving end. This problem is greatly overcome by using **digital** signals for transmission.

Non-Equivalence Gate (NEQ) This is a **logic gate** which operates with **binary digits** and is also known as the **exclusive–OR gate**. Its output is of logic value 0 only when all its inputs are the same. (Note that with an **inclusive–OR gate** the output is of logic value 1 when any of its inputs has a logic value 1). For example: with a two-input NEQ or X–OR gate the following **truth table** applies.

Input		Output
0	0	0
0	1	1
1	0	1
1	1	0

a NEQ or X–OR gate

This gate could be used to find whether or not two binary digits are the same: it could also be used to sum two binary digits but it does not give the carry digit (that is, when adding $1 + 1$ in **binary notation** we get 10 where the 1 is the carry digit and the 0 is the sum).

NOR Gate   A **logic gate** the same as **NOT OR** (Not OR) which operates with **binary digits**. Its output is of logic value 1 only when all its inputs have a logic value 0 otherwise it is 1.

For example: with a two input NOR gate the following **truth table** applies.

Input		Output
0	0	1
0	1	0
1	0	0
1	1	0

a NOR gate

Normalise When working with **floating point arithmetic** it is necessary to adjust each number so that it has the required number of digits after the point. The number is then said to be normalised.

NOT Gate This is a **logic gate** sometimes known as an 'inverter'. The output is always the opposite of the input.

Input	Output
0	1
1	0

a NOT gate

When combined with an **AND** or an **OR gate** it inverts the output to give a **NAND** or a **NOR gate** respectively.

131

n-Type The way in which a **semiconductor** such as **silicon** conducts electricity can be changed greatly by adding a small amount of an impurity. Some impurities such as arsenic increase the number of electrons ('n' means more negative) and thus give n-type silicon. Transistors are made by combining n-type and **p-type** materials together.

Number Cruncher The name given to computers (usually **mainframe**) whose task is to carry out large mathematical calculations.

Numeric Referring to numbers. In **denary notation** this would use the digits 0 to 9. A numeric **keyboard** would have ten keys, one for each number.

```
7 8 9
4 5 6
1 2 3
  0
```

Object Code   A program written in a **high level language** is called a **source** program. A **compiler**, with or without an **assembler**, is used to produce a binary version of the source program in object code. This is in fact **machine code** which the computer understands and contains **data** as well as **instructions**.

Octal Notation   In this system one counts in 'eights' instead of 'tens' using the digits 0 to 7. Whereas the three positions in denary represent hundreds, tens and units, in octal they represent 64's, 8's and 1's.

For example:

$$764 \text{ in octal} = (7 \times 64) + (6 \times 8) + (4 \times 1)$$
$$= 448 \quad + \quad 48 + \quad 4$$
$$= 500 \text{ in denary}$$

To change from octal to **binary notation** each digit is converted in turn. 7 is 111, 6 is 110 and 4 is 100. So

$$764 \text{ in octal} = 111110100 \text{ in binary}$$

(Check
$256 + 128 + 64 + 32 + 16 + 0 + 4 + 0 + 0 = 500$)

On/Off Line A term used to describe whether or not a terminal user is connected to the computer. Often terminals off line are used for **data** preparation though if they have their own processor they can operate as an independent computer.

Operation Code The part of a **machine code** instruction which says what has to be done has, itself, to be coded. The code used is called the operation code and although it is in **numeric** form it would mean such things as 'print', 'add' and 'subtract'.

For example: the operation code for 'print' might be 13 and so to print the contents of **location** 17 a programmer might code

| 13 | 0017 | or | 13 | 17 |

However in **binary notation** this would be

| 00001101 | 0000000000010001 |

Optical Character Recognition (OCR) A device which is able to recognise normal **characters** like A, B, 6, ? and provide corresponding input to a computer. At the present time such a machine would have difficulty in reading handwriting though certain types of print are easily read.

For example: the following are OCR characters

Operand A **machine code** instruction can be divided into two parts. First the operator (using an **operation code**) controls the process to be done (this might be print or load the **accumulator**). Second the operand controls which memory **locations** are used and, for example, to which port or device the **data** is to be sent.

For example: a machine code instruction

136

using a 24-bit **word** might be arranged in 8
and 16 bits

★★★★★★★★	★★★★★★★★★★★★★★★★

OPERATOR   OPERAND
8 bits   16 bits
255 processes   65536 different addresses

Operating System This is the program
which supervises the running of other programs. In a large computer the operating
system selects which program to run at which
time according to their importance and the
availability of **peripherals**. It also controls
the use of these external units such as **card
readers**, **printers** and **backing store**. For a
microcomputer the operating system might
permit such commands as 'load', 'run',
'merge', 'list' and 'save'. A well-known
system for use with Z80 **microprocessor**
computers is CP/M (control program for
microcomputer) developed by an American
company who hold the copyright.

Optical Disk This disk which is read by
using a light (laser) beam is used for storing

data. Changes in the way the light beam is reflected as the disk revolves are used to provide binary code for **video** playback on a television screen or a computer.

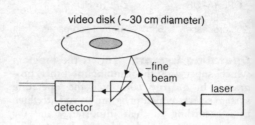

video disk (~30 cm diameter)

fine beam

laser

detector

Optical Mark Reader This device does no more than detect the presence or absence of a pencil mark in certain places on sheets of paper or computer cards. It is sometimes guided as to the positions to be read by clock marks (thick black lines) printed down one edge. Examination Boards often use an optical mark reader to record candidates' answers to multichoice type questions.

Oracle The name of the IBA's **teletext** service which transmits **data** along with the normal television programme transmissions. Each page is transmitted in turn in a never-ending sequence as a form of 'dots' tucked away out of sight at the top of the television screen. With a teletext decoder this data can be made to fill the screen (or be superimposed over the picture) one page at a time. Oracle includes advertising pages and provides local information by transmitting a selection of different pages in different regions. The data of page 175 onwards when loaded into particular **microcomputers** provides **software** for those machines. Software transmitted in this way is known as **telesoftware**.

OR Gate This is a **logic gate** which operates with **binary digits**. Its output is of logic value 1 when any of its inputs have logic value 1.

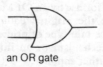

an OR gate

For example: with a two input OR gate the following **truth table** applies

Input		Output
0	0	0
0	1	1
1	0	1
1	1	1

This is the **inclusive-OR gate** as opposed to the **exclusive-OR** or **non-equivalence gate** which gives 0 if 'all' the inputs have logic value 1.

Original Equipment Manufacturer (OEM)

A term used to describe the manufacturer who makes and sells a piece of equipment which may include products of other manufacturers. Thus these other manufacturers would point out that their products were suitable for use by an OEM.

For example: the original equipment manufacturer of a certain type of printer might use a print-head mechanism or an **integrated circuit** from another supplier.

Output The name given to the available results of the computer's work. It may be sheets and sheets of paper on to which the results have been printed or it might take the form of a picture on a television or **monitor** screen. Other examples of an output device include a **graph plotter**, **card punch**, **paper tape** punch and **microfiche**.

Overflow When a computer carries out arithmetic, say adding two numbers together, it is possible for the answer to be too big for the computer to store in the space allowed. The term overflow is used to describe this situation though generally a computer signals the problem to the user when it happens. Overflow is much more likely to occur with **fixed point arithmetic** than with **floating point arithmetic** the latter being able to store numbers up to 10^{38} using two 8-bit words. That is a number in **denary notation** with thirty-eight noughts.

Overlay A useful way of overcoming the problem of not having enough **main store** in a computer. The **program**, which is too long, is loaded and run in sections, more of the program being called into memory as and when required. Each new section overlays and rubs out a previous section.

Packing Density A measure of the amount of **data** that can be held by a **backing store** usually stated as so many **bytes** or so many **bits** per unit length.

For example: 800 bits/inch for half-inch magnetic tape.

Page Often used to mean a full screen of **data** as displayed by a **monitor**, though sometimes as with **Prestel**, each full screen is called a **frame** and a page consists of several frames. 'Paging' is the switching between blocks of computer memory and **radio paging** is a British Telecom service.

Paper Tape Computer paper tape is usually 2½ centimetres wide and comes in rolls 250 metres long. It is punched, one **character** at a time, with a row of holes; four rows per centimetre length. Each row has the same number of possible holes which can be 5, 6, 7 or 8. Eight-track tape is divided 5 to 3 by the **sprocket holes** which are punched at the same time and are used to guide the tape through the reader. Being off-centre the tape cannot be fed in upside down.

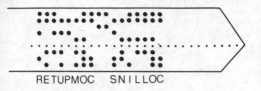

RETUPMOC SNILLOC

This type of coding can be read at 1500 characters per second by a paper tape reader.

Parallel Transmission This requires at least as many wires or paths as there are **bits** to be transmitted at the same time. With 8-bit **words** all the eight bits of each word would be transferred in parallel along eight paths at the same time.

For example: imagine six rows of soldiers each row having eight men in each. To move this block forward each row could move in turn, eight men moving 'parallel' to one another.

145

Alternatively the man at the left of each row could lead and his row could follow in line or 'serially'.

In terms of electrical transmission this would require just one wire but in fact both systems would have parity checks and **handshake**.

Parameter Often in the course of carrying out a **program** (or a procedure) the computer does different tasks depending on the value of something or on the particular key that was last pressed. Such values which have a particular meaning to the computer are called parameters.

Parity Bit This extra bit is included with a set of **binary digits** as a check to see that all the binary digits are transferred correctly. Its value is 0 or 1 depending on the values of the other digits. If the number of 1's, including the parity bit, is even then the word has even parity: if the number of 1's is odd then it has odd parity.

Pascal Blaise Pascal (French 1623–1662). He designed and built in 1642 a toothed gear-wheel machine that could do both addition and subtraction; the first mechanical **calculator**. Also PASCAL is the name of a high level programming language developed in the early 1970's as a teaching language. Today it is used for general purpose programming.

Password A group of **characters** correctly given when demanded by a computer allows access by the user.

Peripheral A device that can be connected and controlled by a computer but external to the CPU.
For example: a **card reader**, a disk drive, a **bar code** reader, **joy sticks**, games paddles and **visual display units** (VDU's).

Pilot A computer programming language specifically designed for creating **computer assisted learning** (CAL) packages. It has fourteen simple commands allowing the author to create sets of questions with routing for the student depending on the answers given.

Pixel These are the tiny areas (dots or PICture ELements) that make up a computer graphics picture. The smaller each pixel, the greater their number and the higher the resolution of the picture (more detail can be seen). However the variation in brightness and the number of colours depend on the **bits** per pixel.

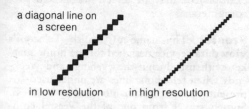

a diagonal line on a screen

in low resolution   in high resolution

For example: on a **monitor screen** 600 by 250 pixels may allow only two colours (black and white), whereas 300 by 200 pixels might allow four colours and 150 by 100, sixteen colours.

PL/1 A **high level language** designed with the intention of combining the problem solving facilities of **FORTRAN** with the **data**-handling capabilities of **COBOL**.

Point-of-Sale In a shop or wholesale suppliers this is the place where the goods change hands. When you pay at the till the item becomes yours and any record, such as a stock control figure, needs to be changed at this point. A point-of-sale **terminal** may have its own backing store (magnetic cassette tape for

149

example) or may be directly connected to a computer.

Prestel The name of British Telecom's **viewdata** service designed for the home market with use during the evenings and weekends when telephone lines are under used. At present, though, it is mainly used by business. Signals travel from one of the Prestel computers (all of which are linked) via telephone to a television screen. Nearly 200,000 different pages are available and these cover topics as wide apart as the selection of wines and British Rail train timetables. Information Providers (IP's) buy pages to display their goods or **information**. Users have to pay both telephone line charge and computer time charge when using the system and may also have to pay a page charge which is collected by British Telecom for the Information Providers. Most pages however have a zero page charge and it is possible to access other private viewdata systems through Prestel. Some pages consist of computer **software** and by connecting British Telecom approved **microcomputers** via approved MODEMS one can access this **telesoftware**.

150

Printed Circuit Board A thin board on which electronic components are fixed by solder. Often the component wires are pushed through from one side and soldered on the other side which has the printed circuit. The printed circuit consists of metal strips which connect one component to another. Several such boards might be used in a **microcomputer**, one having the **microprocessor**, another having sets of memory **chips** and others for **high resolution graphics**, controlling the disk drives and so on. Such a set of boards might all plug into a **mother board** or be connected by a cable with many wires.

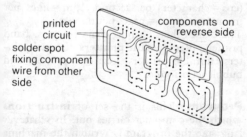

printed circuit

components on reverse side

solder spot fixing component wire from other side

Note that many more intricate connections are

possible with a printed circuit board than with a wired circuit. In fact double sided printed circuit boards are also available.

Printer This device or **peripheral** is used to obtain **hard copy** of the output from a computer. The most common forms of printer are:

teleprinter	10–30 cps
daisywheel printer	50 cps
matrix printer	80 cps
ink-jet printer	200 cps
line printer	1000 1pm
xerographic laser printer	20 ppm

(cps = characters per second, 1pm = lines per minute and ppm = pages per minute).

There are others such as chain printers, band printers, **electrostatic printers**, thermal printers, thimble printers, golf ball printers and bubble jet printers.

Program This is the set of **instructions** which the computer carries out. In whatever language the program is written the machine follows the instructions one at a time in order.

There are five main steps in writing a program:

1) Understanding and solving the problem
2) Flowchart or plan of the solution
3) Coding the program
4) Writing the documentation
5) Trials for testing

With a **top down** approach to **structured programming** the first three steps would be applied to sections at a time resulting in a set of programs each having a particular problem to solve.

Programmable Read Only Memory (PROM) This is similar to a ROM **chip** whose non-**volatile memory** is used to store a fixed program. Using a special **hardware** device it is possible to create one's own ROM using a PROM, but unlike an EPROM it cannot then be changed.

Programmed Learning Not something one would expect in a computing book particularly as it never became widely used despite a great deal of publicity. The idea was

153

that self-study at one's own rate was possible and that direction to the next piece of work could be based on the results or answers to the questions of the previous piece. Now with computers the student has the advantage of an interactive medium capable of storing the progress made and presenting the right piece of work at the right time. **Computer managed learning** (CML) is proving very successful for training in both commerce and industry and with a record-keeping element could do much to assist our educational system.

Programming Language This is the language that allows the computer user to tell the computer what to do. There are many different languages some of which are mentioned in this 'GEM'. Under the general heading of **high level languages** one might include **ALGOL**, **FORTRAN**, **COBAL**, **BASIC** and **PASCAL**. **Machine code** or the manufacturer's **assembler** would be **low level languages**.

Prompt The way in which the computer gives its operator a message. It may be a symbol (e.g. >) or a sentence on a screen or

a coloured light on the keyboard.
For example:

Pseudo-Random Sequence of Numbers

When the computer is asked to generate a **random number** it does so by carrying out a set of **instructions**. The numbers produced can be taken as being random but it is possible to repeat the process starting in the same way and to obtain the same set of random numbers. Only if one can involve some other changing factor, such as the 'time' since switching on, can this partly be overcome.

p-Type The way in which a **semiconductor** such as **silicon** conducts electricity can be changed greatly by adding a small amount of an impurity. Some impurities such as phosphorus have a lack of electrons ('p' means more positive) and this gives us p-type silicon. Transistors are made by combining p-type and **n-type** materials together.

Punched Card Made of thin card this is used to store **data** which is read by detecting the positions of the holes that have been punched. The most common card has eighty columns and measures about 18 cm by 8 cm. There are twelve punching positions in each column and, generally, one particular hole is used for the digits 0 to 9 and a combination of two holes for the other **characters**. A few card codes use three holes in one column.

For example: the 80-column card which uses the 12-bit **Hollerith** code.

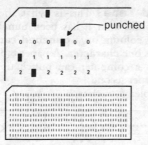

The 96-column card is in fact smaller than the 80-column card and uses round holes rather than rectangular ones. Designed for use in small businesses it can hold about 20% more data.

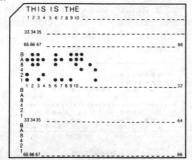

157

Punched Tape This is what the **paper tape** becomes after it has been punched. As with each column on a **punched card**, each row stores one **character**. A paper tape punch driven by a computer can punch up to 100 characters per second.

For example: 5-track tape.

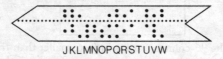

JKLMNOPQRSTUVW

As there are only thirty-two possible ways of punching five holes a letter code punch (all five holes punch) precedes a section of tape with letters and a figure code punch precedes all other characters. In this way ten of the punching combinations can be used for both letters and numbers.

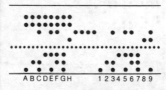

ABCDEFGH 123456789

8-track tape

158

Note that this 8-track code has an odd-**parity bit**. The fourth row is a check row and is punched (or not) so as to make the number of holes punched in a row (or **frame**) odd.

QWERTY This is used to describe the keyboard on a normal two-handed typewriter. The word comes from the first six keys on the second row of the keyboard.

It is interesting to note that the layout of the keys was designed not for speed as we might wish today, but for the opposite. Letters used often were positioned so as to allow time for the hammer to fall back to its place without being hit by the hammer of the next **character**.

Radio Paging   A service offered by British Telecom which allows the wearer of the device to be paged by someone who just dials a particular telephone number. The device does no more than 'beep' but it draws to the wearer's attention that someone wishes to make contact. Similar devices have been used by hospital doctors, firemen and factory foremen for some time.

Random Access Memory (RAM)   This is a set of storage **locations** any of which can be accessed directly without having to work through from the first one. Such memories can both be written to and read from and access times are about the same for all locations. We tend to think of **semiconductor** memories as being the equivalent RAM to **core store** though moving **magnetic memories** such as **disk** and drum are also RAM but have greater access times. Semiconductor RAM can be based on the **junction transistor** or the **field effect transistor** (TTL or CMOS). The first offers the faster access but the latter offers both dynamic RAM and static RAM with dynamic being the cheaper but requiring extra logic circuits to check the contents regularly.

Random Numbers   A set of numbers each one picked entirely at random. However this is not truly possible with most machines and we talk of a **pseudo-random sequence of numbers** as being produced by a **microcomputer**.

Read Only Memory (ROM)   A **memory** that holds **data** or **instructions** permanently and cannot be altered by the computer or programmer. The actual content of a ROM is fixed at the time of its manufacture (PROM is fixed using a special device by the user; EPROM can be changed with difficulty by the user).

For example: a **semiconductor** ROM can be used to store **BASIC** in a **microcomputer** or to store the control programs in pocket calculators and other hand-held devices.

Read/Write Memory   As opposed to **read only memory** (ROM), this type of **memory** can be written into, as well as read. It might be **random access memory** (RAM) or a random access disk **file** but **serial access memory**, such as **bubble memory** and magnetic tape, would also be included.

Real Time This is used to describe a computer system which accepts **data** and updates its records at that time (in real time) feeding back results almost immediately. This in turn has an effect on the next set of data available unlike a **point-of-sale backing store** which may only be accessed by the computer once a day.

For example: an air-line booking system is accessed by remote **terminals**. On receiving a booking it checks that it is available and if so updates its records and confirms the acceptance. From that time other users will find that booking is not available.

Re-Boot A term instructing the user to **bootstrap** the system again. Often used when the **program** has gone wrong or is in an endless loop from which it cannot leave. Also used as a way of changing the program stored in a **microcomputer**; re-boot and re-load.

Register A special type of store **location** in a computer used for a specific purpose. Generally registers are one or two **word**-lengths of the computer.

For example: one register might be used as the

accumulator; another as the **store** address register.

Remote Control   At present such devices are used to operate television receivers, video recorders and some **Prestel** sets. Using a weak, infra-red beam (like a light beam but one that is not detected by our eyes) these gadgets enable a person to operate the machine from various distances with a hand-held keypad. In a similar way one could operate a computer from the comfort of an arm-chair.

Remote Job Entry (RJE)   In **batch processing** the programs that have to be put into the computer may be entered at the computer site or from a number of remote sites. Remote job entry refers to the latter case.

Re-Run   To **run** the computer **program** again with the original **data** starting from the beginning.

Reserved Word   This is generally a **word** which has a specific meaning to the **compiler** and thus must not be used by the programmer when programming in the **high level language**.

Response Time The time taken for a computer to answer after the last key is pressed. This time would be very short in the case of a **microcomputer** but varies greatly when accessing a **mainframe** computer from a **terminal**. The time includes transmission in both directions and would depend on the number of other users.

Right Justification This is the arranging of lines of text so as to **justify** the right-hand edges and make them all in line. However it can also refer to **data** stored in consecutive locations all of which have been filled from the right and may have a different number of spaces on the left.

Right Shift In this operation all the **characters** in a particular **string** are moved one place to the right. If a number is involved then this would have the effect of division.
For example: just as shifting a denary number one place to the right has the effect of dividing by ten so a binary number is divided by two.

| in denary 768.0 | becomes 76.8 |
| in binary 11010 (=26) | becomes 1101 (=13) |

Robotics   The linking of electronics and **microelectronics** with machines enabling complicated and repetitive tasks to be done automatically without human involvement. As machines become more 'intelligent' so more intricate work can be carried out.

Rogue Value   When **data**, such as a series of numbers, is being put into a computer a rogue value is given at the end to show that there are no more numbers.

For example: when putting in a set of values which are the ages in years of a group of people the value 999 might be used as the rogue value. It must not be possible for the rogue value to appear as one of the set.

Rounding   This is one way of reducing a number to a certain number of digits. In **denary notation** if the last digit removed from the right-hand side is a 5 or above the last figure remaining is increased by one.

For example: rounding the number 672.87 to four figures would give 672.9; rounding to three figures would give 673; to two figures would give 670. On the other hand **truncation** to four figures would give 672.8.

Routine This refers to a piece of **software** that does a specific task though generally is also part of a **program**. However the word **subroutine** is often used to describe a self-contained section of a program.

Run Often this word is used as a command to tell the computer to carry out a program though it can imply the loading, the execution and the output of a whole package. The 'run-time' is a measure of the time taken for the whole program to be carried out.

Scheduling   This is the arranging of the order in which programs are to be run and may be done by the computer itself.

For example: it may not be possible to run the first program in a queue if it requires more memory than is available at that time. Even programs that are running sometimes let others go ahead if a certain **peripheral**, say a **printer**, is not free when required.

Schema   This word refers to an outline description or diagram of a **database** that can be accessed by the computer.

Scratch Pad Memory   Just as we might use a scratch pad for working out, say, the cost of 24 pens at 17p each so the computer may reserve an area of **memory** for holding results

of calculations that it will need later.

Screen This is the front of a television set, **visual display unit** (VDU) or **monitor** and is used for displaying computer text and graphics.

'Screen copy' refers to the output from a computer as seen on a screen;

'screen editor' refers to the editing facilities offered to the user by a **terminal** screen; and

'screen memory' refers to the memory available to the computer or the user in the terminal itself.

Scroll This is the continuous movement of the display on the **screen** where generally as one line is added at the bottom all lines move up one and the line at the top disappears from view. Most **microcomputers** can be set to scroll either one page at a time (one screenful) or continuously. Horizontal scrolling is used with some **word processors**. Here, should the line length be greater than the screen width then on reaching the right-hand side of the screen the whole display moves to the left. Some **text editor** type programs only move the particular line to the left.

Search Whereas it would be far too time consuming for us to search a large set of records for particular items this is in fact one thing that a computer can do very quickly. In a search, each item would be accessed and checked in turn by the program which would only select those required.

Second Generation Computers These computers built between the mid 1950's and the mid 1960's used transistors. Thus they were smaller, more reliable and required less power than the **first generation computers** which used electronic **valves**.

Sector A magnetic **disk** or drum uses circular tracks for storing **data**. These tracks

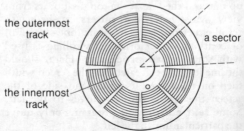

the outermost track

a sector

the innermost track

are **format**ted into sectors and the computer writes data, one sector track at a time, from its memory. Note that although the length of a track in a sector near the centre of a **mini-floppy disk** is shorter it holds the same amount of data as those further out.

Seed Crystal This is a small single crystal which when held in its own supersaturated solution grows into a large crystal.

For example: a small **silicon** seed crystal is rotated and slowly withdrawn from molten silicon to give the cylindrical crystal from which silicon **wafers** are cut.

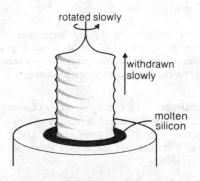

rotated slowly

withdrawn slowly

molten silicon

Segmented Program This is a computer **program** written in sections which are called up from **backing store** as and when required. One section would probably **overlay** the previous section in the **main store**.

Semiconductor This is a material which is neither a good conductor of electricity like copper nor a good insulator like plastic. It is somewhere between the two and the way in which it conducts electricity can be changed by adding (called 'doping') a small amount of another substance (an impurity).

For example: **silicon** is a semiconductor; doping it with a small amount of arsenic provides extra negative electrons giving what is known as **n-type** silicon; doping with phosphorus provides a lack of electrons giving **p-type**. Other semiconductors include **germanium** and the compound **gallium arsenide**.

Sentinel The name given to a **character** or set of characters which have a special meaning which is usually that they are the last item of **data**. **Terminator** and **rogue value** are other words used.

For example: in a microcomputer program which accepts a series of positive numbers it may be that on finding a negative number (the sentinel or indicator) the program knows that it has the complete series.

Serial Access Memory This **read/write memory** is a set of **locations** which can only be accessed in sequence.
For example: to read a particular record stored on a magnetic tape it would be necessary to go through all the records in sequence until it is found. Another example is **bubble memory** though here **access times** would be shorter.

Serial Transmission This method is where each **character** or piece of **data** is transmitted in order, one after the other along a wire rather than having one wire for each bit as in **parallel transmission**. Certain standard interfaces have been defined for serial ports and these include RS232, V24 and RS423.

Seven Segment Display Used with **light emitting diodes** and **liquid crystal displays** to show the numbers 0 to 9. Generally the seven segments, a, b, c, d, e, f and g lean slightly to the right.

The patterns are:

1 2 3 4 5

6 7 8 9

Shared Files These are files held in the memory of one computer either in **immediate access store** or in **backing store** which can be read, used and altered by other computers.

Shift Register This is a **location** in the computer which is used only for shifting **data** to the left or right. Note that a shift one place to the left on a denary number is like multiplying by ten, though the first digit of the number is lost if it filled the location completely.

For example: with a denary number

| 0 | 4 | 7 | 2 |

Shift left is like multiplying by 10

| 4 | 7 | 2 | 0 |

Shift right is like dividing by 10

| 0 | 0 | 4 | 7 |

In **binary notation**

| 0 | 1 | 1 | 0 | (=6)

Shift left is like multiplying by 2

| 1 | 1 | 0 | 0 | (=12)

Shift right is like dividing by 2

| 0 | 0 | 1 | 1 | (=3)

Signal This is a way of using electricity to convey **data** along a cable or through an electronic system. The change may be in the current flowing or the voltage used. In an analogue signal the change can have any value but with a digital signal there are only two values (interpreted as a 0 or 1).

For example: a common standard for serial transmission is RS232C where a 0 is less than −6 volts and a 1 is greater than +6 volts.

Sign Bit With 8–**bit** words usually seven bits are used to represent the number and the eighth, the sign: 0 for positive and 1 for negative. In the commonly used **two's com-**

plement notation only the first digit is negative and this indicates the sign.

For example:

| 0 1000001 | would be | +65 |

| 1 0011011 | would be | −101 |

In **floating point arithmetic** a second 8-bit word for each number would give the position of the 'bicimal' point.

Silicon A cheap and widely available **semiconductor** material that has replaced **germanium** in most electronic **solid state devices**. Although it is the second most abundant element (after oxygen) on the Earth's surface it does not occur naturally. Sand and quartz are natural forms of silica (silicon dioxide) from which silicon is obtained.

Simplex Operation Unlike **duplex operation** this mode of transmission allows **data** to travel in only one direction. A terminal that communicates with a computer via such a channel can either send or receive but not both. Duplex allows travel in both directions at the same time; half-duplex allows travel in both directions but not at the same time.

For example: simplex transmission could be from the **keyboard** of a **terminal** to its computer 'or' from the computer to the **visual display unit** screen of the terminal.

Simulation Is the representation of a situation by a computer system such that the decisions and actions of the user cause the same effects and results as when carried out for real. This mode of use of a computer assists training, particularly where mistakes in the real situation would be too costly or too dangerous.

For example: learning to fly a helicopter or operating a nuclear power station.

Small Scale Integration (SSI) This is a measure of the number of **logic gates** on a single **chip** (about one half centimetre square).

Small scale integration (SSI)	less than 20
Medium scale integration (MSI)	20 to 100
Large scale integration (LSI)	100 to 5000
Very large scale integration (VLSI)	over 5000

Soft Sectored This describes the way in which the length of a **sector** is fixed on a **floppy disk**. In this case the length is set by the **microcomputer** when the disk is for-matted. Soft sectored floppy disks are distinguished from **hard sectored** ones by the fact that they have only a single hole near the centre hole of the disk (hard sectored have a ring of say 6 or 12).

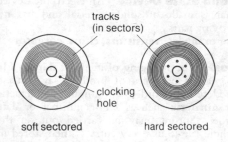

tracks
(in sectors)

clocking
hole

soft sectored   hard sectored

Software Software, as opposed to **hardware**, refers to all the **programs** that can be run on a particular computer. It would include the **operating system**, the **assemblers,** the **compilers** and all the software packages (specific programs for specific tasks) that are available. Software Houses are companies that write and supply software packages for computer systems; thus one does not have to buy all software from the computer manufacturer.

Solid State Device An electronic device that is made of solid material and has no moving parts.
For example: **transistors**, **chips**, **core store**.

Sort The arranging of items of **data** (a **file** of names or types of product say) into a predetermined order. This might be alphabetic or **numeric** such as house number or date order. Sorting may be carried out on the whole file (thus every entry is then stored in sequence) or may be done only on those items selected for printing. A computer sorts by comparing the items of data, two at a time and exchanging their positions in memory if necessary. Different methods of sorting (e.g.

bubble sort, shell sort) make the comparisons in different orders and sometimes the sort is only carried out on part of the record. **Inverted files** are sorted on a particular part of each record and although the sorting ('file inversion') is very time consuming, in use such files are quickly accessed.

Source Language This is the language in which the programmer writes his **program** (the source program) though it cannot be directly understood by a computer. Either the source program is converted to an object program (**machine code** which can be run directly by the computer) using a **compiler** or it is run one line at a time using an **interpreter**.

For example: BASIC, COBOL, ALGOL are all examples of source languages.

Speech Recognition This is the interpretation by a computer of the spoken word. Already in use are machines that respond to words though the vocabulary is limited and the pronunciation must be clear. Development at present is limited by processor speeds and memory sizes.

Speech Synthesiser This is the generation of speech by **solid state** circuits. Used in hand-held educational machines and toys where a limited vocabulary is required. At present there is a noticeable difference between machine and human speech but more variation in machine accent is becoming available.

Sprocket Holes These appear as a series of holes along punched paper tape and along the edges of **continuous stationery**. In both cases they are used to feed the item automatically through a device.

For example: paper tape.

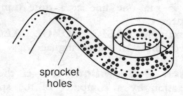

sprocket
holes

Stack A temporary area of **memory** used to hold sets of **data**. As each item is added the previous ones are all shifted down one place – thus they are thought of as being 'stacked' one above the other. New items are added at the end and only the end one can be removed at any time (i.e. last in first out).

Stationery Computer stationery is usually of the **continuous stationery** type which consists of fan-folded pages joined by perforations and having **sprocket holes** along the edges. These forms may be pre-printed with the name of the company or organisation, leaving space on each page for the computer print. Sets of single sheets can be printed using single-sheet feeders.

Stepping Motor As opposed to an ordinary electric motor this turns a step at a time with, say, 96 steps for one revolution. The number of steps is fixed by the manufacturer and depends on both the number of sets of coils and the number of coils in each set. With 4 sets each having 12 coils, 48 positions are possible and 96 steps can be achieved by holding half-way between positions. It is moved from one position to the next by activating different sets of coils in turn, using a sequence of numbers which can be provided by the digital **output** of a computer. This is an important method of producing precise movement under **microprocessor** control and is widely used in **robotics.**

Store This is the name given to anything that can retain **data** given to it by the **central processing unit** of a computer. **Core store**, memory **chips**, **bubble memory**, magnetic **disk**, drum and **tape** are all types of store. The number of binary **bits** in each memory location of the store depends on the design of the computer. Generally **microcomputers** use 8 or 16 bits, **mainframe** computers use 24, 32 or 48 bits. The size of the store is the number of memory locations; 64K would be 65535 ($2^{16}-1$). A **character** usually occupies 8 bits so each memory location could contain one or two or three or more characters depending on the computer. When **immediate access store** was expensive 6 bits were used for each character though this allowed no codes for graphics.

String Bearing in mind the old adage 'How long is a piece of string?' the computer uses this word to describe a set of **characters** which may in fact only be one character. Whereas numbers are stored in fixed length memories, the spaces being filled with zeros, characters are used in groups of various lengths. They are stored in a series of memory **locations** with the first location holding a number giving the length of the string (the number of characters). BASIC uses the dollar ($) symbol next to the **variable** to denote that it is a string.

For example: A$ = 'HELLO' and this word might be stored in six locations, the first holding the number 5.

Structured Programming This is the art of writing **programs** that are logical and easy to follow. It involves the sectioning of the original problem into small program units each of which is self-contained and can be tested separately. The main program can then consist of a series of **instructions** each sending the computer to a particular unit or **subroutine** which it carries out and then returns. In addition instructions such as FOR . . . NEXT, REPEAT . . . UNTIL and DO . . . WHILE . . . allow easy structuring in program writing. With a **top down** approach the program is written in units in the same way as the problem was originally solved and it can be argued that **flowcharts** are not required with this method. However the programming needs to be extremely well structured.

Subroutine This is a section of a **program** written to carry out a specific task which the main program may use just once or several times during its run. The last **instruction** of a subroutine usually returns the computer to the instruction following the one from which it left the main program. Large computer systems have a set of subroutines on disk or tape which can be 'called' and used by the current program as and when required. A 'procedure' is a form of subroutine in that the programmer can use it once or several times during a program. The main difference is that it is 'called' by name and must be defined (written) outside the main body of the program. It can also have its own **variables**.

Synchronous Mode This is the performance of a computer whereby the start of every operation is dependent on a pulse from its internal clock. Thus the completion of one task does not signal the start of the next as in

asynchronous mode – the machine waits, albeit for a fraction of a second, for the next clock pulse.

Syntax Just as the words we speak need to be in a certain grammatical order to be understood so the **instructions** to a computer must obey certain rules. 'Syntax error' is stated by the machine when instruction errors have been made by the programmer.

For example: the instruction

10 INPUT A;B

in BASIC would give a syntax error because it should be

10 INPUT A,B

and the rules for writing program instructions have not been obeyed.

System This is the total of all the things that make up the working computer unit. It includes **hardware** (the computer itself plus all the **peripheral** units), **software** and the necessary **data** and operators.

189

System Analysis This is the evaluation coupled if necessary with the design and installation of a computer system to solve a problem. Several stages are involved.
1) Analysis of how the job is done at present.
2) Deciding if a computer can be of use
3) Breaking down the problem into logical steps, designing a solution and specifying exactly what the computer must do.
4) Installing the computer system and seeing it works as required.

System X The name of British Telecom's digital **telecommunications** system. Speech from a telephone is converted into digital **data** (0's and 1's) and these digital signals are transmitted as opposed to the continuously varying analogue **signals** as at present. Such signals can also be sent via **fibre optics** cables.

Table In science work, results from experiments are sometimes recorded in a table of values. Temperature and time readings as a liquid cools might be listed in two columns,

Temperature/C	Time/s
72	0
60	30
51	60
44	90
38	120
33	150

Such results could be stored as an **array** in a computer memory as

(72,0) (60,30) (51,60) (44,90)   and so on

This arrangement of **data** in rows and columns is called a table. In addition items in such a table can be easily located by means of a **look-up table** which directs the computer without its having to search every item.

Tabulator The name given to the calculating equipment available from 1890 to about 1960. **Hollerith** built the first tabulator which read and counted the 1890 USA census figures from **punch cards**. Others could be programmed by making wire connections between holes on a control panel.

Tape A long strip of paper or magnetic coated plastic which is used to record **data**. **Paper tape** can use 5, 6, 7 or 8 holes to represent each **character** and half-inch magnetic tape similarly uses 7 or 9 channels across its width. (Audio cassette tape records **bits** serially one after the other). One difference with magnetic tape is that data is usually stored in blocks and that in addition to checking the **parity bit** of each character the computer checks each block as it is read.

Telecommunications The sending of **data** from one place to another by radio waves or cables. Note the derivative of this word in the title 'British Telecom'.

Teleprinter Teleprinters and teletypewriters are devices similar to typewriters. Teleprinters were originally designed to send and receive messages transmitted serially using a telephone line and a 5-**bit** code.

Teletypewriters usually work with the 8-bit **ASCII code** and are used specifically for sending and receiving messages to and from computer systems.

Both can have a tape reader and punch attached so that tapes can be prepared **off line** and read at a later time. As an **output** device they usually work at 10 or 30 characters per second and suitably adapted they make a cheap but slow secondhand printer for a **microcomputer**.

Telesoftware This describes the transmission of computer **software** from one computer to another by **telecommunications**. At present telesoftware is available on both the BBC's and IBA's **teletext** services and British Telecom's **Prestel** system, though radio transmissions are also being tried. **Ceefax** page 700 onwards, **Oracle** page 175 onwards and Prestel, details given on page 2114.

Teletext An information service transmitted as part of the normal television signal. Each page is transmitted in turn in a never ending sequence as a form of 'dots' tucked away out of sight at the top of the television screen. If the receiving set is fitted with a teletext decoder these top four lines of the picture can be made to fill the whole screen. The user selects the page number and that page is decoded the next time it is transmitted. Information available varies from pages on news and sport to food prices and film reviews. IBA's version of teletext is called **Oracle** and the BBC's is called **Ceefax**. Uses of teletext now include advertising, local information and **telesoftware**.

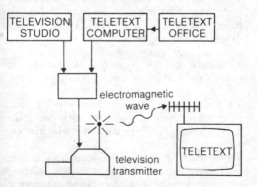

Television Receiver This is the television set most people have in their home. It normally receives a transmitted signal via an aerial or cable and converts this radio frequency (RF) signal (or more precisely UHF signal) into picture plus colour and sound. Most **microcomputers** have a socket which gives a signal suitable for displaying the **output** on a television receiver but it is necessary to 'tune' the set to the required channel the first time this is done. Some sets are receiver/**monitor** and these have a second input socket which accepts a **video** signal from a microcomputer. This provides a better quality picture particularly when displaying detailed graphics. For the clearest quality colour picture the red, green and blue signals are sent separately and this requires a RGB computer output and a RGB monitor.

Telex The name given to the service which allows users to communicate with each other using the telephone system and a **teleprinter**.

Terminal A device connected to a computer that allows input and output of **data**. A terminal may be just a keyboard, a teletypewriter (like a **teleprinter**) or a **visual display unit** (VDU) and is often remote from the computer.

For example: a magnetic stripe card reader, keyboard and display as in a bank cash dispenser or a bar code reader and cash till at a supermarket checkout.

Terminator This, like a **rogue value**, is the last piece of a set of **data** and is used to indicate to the computer that it is the last item. Similarly terminators are used on **punched tape** to indicate the end of each record.

Text Editor A piece of software often thought of as a limited word processing package. It can be used to create **files** of text, modify such files and **format** their layout prior to printing. In addition such software allows modification of the order and content of any set of **data** which the computer has created as part of a program. This is a useful way of quickly adding an item in the middle of a set of records thus moving all those below one step down.

Thin Film Memories This is the name of **integrated circuits** (**chips**) made by depositing thin layers in patterns on top of one another. The chips on **silicon wafers** are built a layer at a time, the pattern of each layer being governed by a particular mask. The process by which ultra-violet light is used to define the pattern and thus the circuit is called 'photolithography'. Today X-ray radiation and electron beams are used to define the pattern as with their smaller wavelengths more circuits and thus more memories are possible on the same size chip. **Epitaxy** is another method being used with other **semiconductors** to manufacture thin film memories.

Third Generation Computers These computers were the ones built using **integrated circuits**, the first in 1966. The second generation used **transistors** whilst the first generation used electronic **valves**.

Time Sharing This is the way in which two or more users seem to be using the computer at the same time. In actual fact the computer is dealing with each in turn but to the user it seems that they have sole use.

Output to a **printer** for one user though, could be printed at the same time as the computer does a calculation for another user. Only when the number of time sharing users becomes large does the delay become noticeable.

Top Down This refers to one method of programming whereby the programmer divides the problem into many small units each of which follows on from the one before. A computer **program** is then written for each of these units and tested separately. Only when it runs successfully is it added to the previous one. In this way the final program is built from the top downwards, and it is argued that no **flowchart** is required when using this method. However **structured programming** is required for easy understanding.

Trace The name given to a piece of **software** which follows each step of a **program** line by line. It enables the user to check and locate errors in programs by printing each line number as it carries out that instruction.

Track The name given to the channel or line along which **data** is recorded on a storage device.

For example: the row of holes on **paper tape** or the magnetic line parallel to the edge on magnetic tape.

Tractor Feed The name given to the method of moving paper through a **printer** where it is held by the **sprocket holes** along the two edges. The advantage over friction feed is that when using pre-printed **continuous stationery** the lining-up of the paper and print is far more accurate.

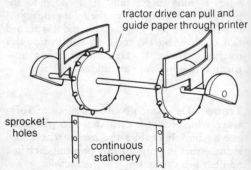

tractor drive can pull and
guide paper through printer

sprocket
holes

continuous
stationery

For example: most small printers offer friction feed (the paper is held by the roller like a typewriter) but tractor feed can be an optional extra.

Transducer Any device that converts energy from an electrical form or to an electrical form.

For example: a loudspeaker is a transducer in that it converts electrical energy into sound energy that we can hear. Other examples include:

    A light sensitive pen in a bar code reader
    An electric motor
    An electrical thermometer

Transistor Invented in 1948 it revolutionised the electronic and computing world by replacing the unreliable **valve**. This **solid state** device is small, reliable, cheap and consumes very little power. It can be used as an amplifier or as a switching device, the latter forming the basis of computer logic and memory circuits. Joining two transistors together leads to **astable** and **bistable** circuits which are the building blocks of today's electronic systems. Transistors are made from **p-type** and **n-type** (n–p–n being the most common) **semiconductors** such as **silicon**, **germanium** and **gallium arsenide**. There are two main types of **transistor**, the **junction transistor** and the **field effect transistor** (FET). The first type, sometimes known as 'bipolar', is the faster acting and more robust of the two though the voltage at which it works is more critical and a stabilised 5V power supply is required. The first **chip** was created in 1959 when a (junction) transistor and resistor were built together, hence the term 'transistor-resistor-logic' or (TRL).

Transistor-Transistor-Logic (TTL)

The **logic circuit** design of joining the **junction** or bipolar transistor together on a **chip** has changed over the years from transistor-resistor-logic (TRL) in 1959 to TTL today. It is now used in the largest family of integrated circuits, the 7400 series, which has more than 100 different chips. However because of its need for a 5V stabilised power supply, it has been replaced in many applications by the other type, CMOS (based on the FET). These operate over a wider voltage range (3V to

15V). use less power and allow more logic gates per chip.

Tree This describes a non-linear method of storing **data** in a computer. One piece of data relates to several other pieces and each one of these then relates to more. The computer tree however is upside down with the branches spreading out downwards.

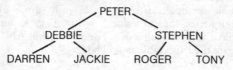

Note that ROGER can be accessed from the root (Peter) as the third piece of data via PETER and STEPHEN. In fact all can be accessed within three. If the names were stored in alphabetical order ROGER would be the fifth piece of data accessed.

Truncation When reducing the number of significant figures in a number, truncation, unlike **rounding**, involves their removal without any consideration of their value.
For example: truncation to three significant

figures of the numbers 56.79 and 23820 would result in the loss of a 9 and 2 respectively.

56.79 would become   56.7
23820 would become 23800

Truth Table This is a table usually filled with 0's and 1's to show the changes carried out by a logical operation such as **AND** or **NOR**.

For example: an AND gate only gives an output of logical value 1 when all its inputs have a logical value of 1. For a two input AND gate the truth table would be:

Input		Output
0	0	0
0	1	0
1	0	0
1	1	1

an AND gate

Turnkey Just as one would expect the door

to open on turning a key so a turnkey system for a microcomputer is one that **bootstraps** and loads the program automatically as soon as one switches on.

Two's Complement   This is a method of holding negative numbers in **binary notation** so that they can be added and subtracted by a computer in the same way as for positive numbers. To calculate $(7-5)$ we could convert the $+5$ to -5 and then add.

$$\text{i.e.} \quad 7+(-5)$$

A similar method can be used with binary numbers by finding the two's **complement**. A number is converted to two's complement by changing all its 0's to 1's and all its 1's to 0's (**negation**) and then adding one. Bearing in mind that in two's complement the place values for the digits are -8, 4, 2 and 1.

Number	1's Complement (negation)	Number in 2's Complement
0101 $(= +5)$	1010	1011 $(= -5)$
0100 $(= +4)$	1011	1100 $(= -4)$
0011 $(= +3)$	1100	1101 $(= -3)$

Subtraction is carried out by finding the two's

complement and then adding.
For example:

$$
\begin{array}{r}
0101 \\
-0011 \\
\hline
\end{array}
\quad \rightarrow \quad
\begin{array}{r}
0101 \\
+1101 \\
\hline
1\underline{0010} = \underline{0010}
\end{array}
$$

as we are working
in 4-bit binary.

(Check $5 - 3 = 2$)

Ultra High Frequency (UHF) A particular range of radio waves having wavelengths approximately between 10 and 100 cm. They are used for television transmissions and as **microcomputer** outputs which connect through the aerial socket for display on a **television receiver**. Frequency values are a few hundred million hertz.

Uncommitted Logic Array (ULA) This is the name given to a **chip** on which there are sets of **logic circuits** that have not yet been connected together. Each set is complete in itself but has to be linked to the others by one or more connections. Thus a chip manufacturer makes his standard ULA

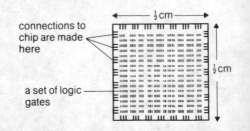

connections to chip are made here

a set of logic gates

½ cm

½ cm

which has the final layer (the circuit pattern) added according to the purchaser's specification. This enables the purchaser (probably an OEM) to obtain their own particular type of chip without the large expense of having one specially designed.

Underflow This is the generation of a number, say by division, which is too small for the computer to store (the computer would in fact store zero). In **floating point notation** using two 8-bit words this would happen when the resulting number was below 10^{-39}. That is a one over a one with thirty-nine noughts.

For example: on a 6-digit **calculator** dividing the number 0.000001 by 2 would give zero. Underflow is the name given when the right-hand digits are lost.

Update This describes the process of changing a file or program package so as to bring it up-to-date. This would include additions of new **data**, changes in data already held and alterations to the program to remove minor errors which have been found. The latter is sometimes called a 'patch'.

For example: an update may be necessary to a payroll package as a result of new Government legislation on PAYE (pay-as-you-earn income tax).

User Group This is a group of people who meet or correspond regularly because of their interest in a particular machine. Most makes of **microcomputers** have their own user groups, generally supported by the manufacturer but controlled by the members. Meetings allow the sharing of both problems and solutions and provide advance information on new products. Much is to be gained at a small cost for all those who become members.

User Port This is a socket on the back of a **microcomputer** that allows the user to connect additional equipment. Often, but not always, it consists of eight **data** lines 'out' and eight 'in' plus particular voltage lines. Numbers that are sent appear in binary.

For example: in 8-**bits** the number 12 would appear on the eight lines as 00001100 where a logical 0 would be 0 volts and a logical 1 between 4.5 and 5.0 volts.

Utility Programs   These are programs designed to perform particular tasks such as listing a **file** held on magnetic **tape** on the printer or copying **data** from one **disk** to another prior to a program run.

Validity Check This is a check that can be written into a **program** by the programmer so that the computer does not accept and use **data** that is wrong.

For example: such a check might be made on records of people's ages ensuring none were negative and none were above say 120. It would also be sensible to check that none consisted of alphabetic **characters**.

Valve An electronic device created around 1900 in which electrodes are enclosed in glass (like a light bulb). Used in radios, television receivers and computers; the first computer had about 18000 valves. The valve has now been largely replaced by the **transistor** and other **semiconductor** devices.

VALVES

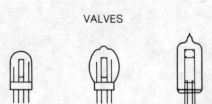

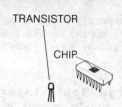

TRANSISTOR

CHIP

Variable The name of **character**(s) used to refer to an area of memory.

For example: if A7 is used as a variable in a **program** and at some point is given the value 21 (A7 = 21) then a specific location referred to as A7 will hold the number 21. An **instruction** to PRINT A7 should result in 21 being printed. Should the variable be a **string** of **characters** then several locations would be used.

Verifier A machine that allows one to check the punching that has previously been done on tape or cards. The operator re-types on a keyboard as the original tape or card is read, the machine checking that the two are the same. When entering **data** via a key to disk system verification is still done by re-typing and comparing but any mistakes can be altered much more easily than with cards or punched tape.

Very Large Scale Integration (VLSI)
As with **large scale integration** (LSI) this is a measure of the number of **logic gates** on a single **chip**. Between 1960 and 1970 designers produced more and more logic gates on a single chip, the number approximately doubling every year from the single gate of 1959. First came **small scale integration** (SSI) with up to 20 logic gates and then **medium scale integration** (MSI) with 20 to 100. By 1969 we had large scale integration with 100 to 5000 logic gates and since 1975 we have had very large scale integration with numbers above 5000 on a chip about a half-centimetre square.

Video Conference
This is the name given to a discussion between two or more groups of people who are in different places but can see and hear each other. Pictures and sound are carried by the **telecommunication**

network and such conferences take place across the world using satellites.

Video Disk A device for storing **data** which looks like a long-playing music record and is used both for television programmes and computer programs. The difference is that it is read without being touched. One method uses a fine laser beam which is reflected by the grooves on the **optical disk** as it revolves. It is the variation in the reflected beam that gives the data stored. At present there are three types of video disk

1) Laser beam type
2) Capacitance type with grooves
3) Capacitance type without grooves

The time taken to access data from a particular part of the disk is less than a hundredth of a millionth of a second.

Video Signal In a television set it is this signal that provides the picture though in the case of a television transmission entering through the aerial socket it has to be separated from the sound. Most **microcomputers** will display their **output** on a television set via the aerial socket though for better picture definition one should use a **monitor** which accepts a video signal (this has a lower frequency than the UHF aerial signal). Some video recorders have a composite video output and for this reason many **television receivers** are now being made with video inputs as well as UHF. For the clearest colour picture however the red, green and blue video signals should be sent separately and this requires both a RGB computer output and a RGB video monitor.

Videotext The name given to any information service which can display text on the screen of a television set. The code may be transmitted as part of a television picture (**teletext**) or as a coded telephone signal (**viewdata**). A typical page has 24 lines with up to 40 characters per line.

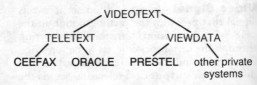

Viewdata An information service transmitted via the telephone lines which provides almost instant access to pages of information. **Prestel** is the name given to British Telecom's public viewdata system though there are many private ones in use. In addition it is possible for the user to communicate with the computer which provides the service and, as in the case of Prestel, place orders for goods and pay for them by quoting credit card numbers.

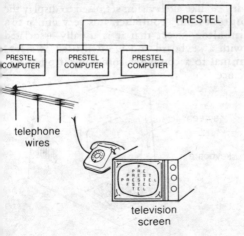

Virtual Memory This is a facility available in large modern computers whereby the programmer is not restricted by the size of the machine's memory. The machine translates virtual **locations** that the programmer has specified into actual locations as and when required using **backing stores** to provide the extra memory space.

Visual Display Unit (VDU) This is a device, like a television set, used to display the **output** from a computer. It is very similar to a **monitor** except that it is usually associated with a keyboard and is often used as a **terminal** to a computer sometimes from a distance.

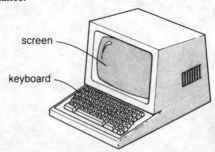

screen

keyboard

Voice Input   This is the operating of a device controlled by a **microprocessor** not by pressing keys on a keyboard but by speech using a microphone. The device may be mechanical, electrical or electronic. At present machines are able to accept a range of words but these do have to be spoken clearly.

Volatile Memory   This refers to all types of **memory** which lose their stored **data** as soon as the power is switched off.
For example: **Core store** and **RAM chips** are volatile whereas magnetic **disk** and **bubble memory** are not.

Wafer The name given to a thin slice cut from a large crystal of **germanium** or **silicon**. First used in the mid 1950's to make **transistors** but led to the **integrated circuit** or **chip** in 1959. A typical wafer would be 0.01 inch thick, 10 cm in diameter and contain 250 chips.

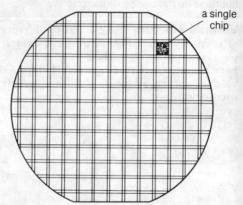

a single chip

Winchester Disk Drive These are designed to take the place of **disk units** for small computers thus avoiding the problems of removing and handling **floppy disks**. These 'hard disks' as they are sometimes called, behave as a fixed disk system with the read/write head being much closer to the disk. In this way the tracks are much closer together and far more **data** can be stored.

For example: a 5¼ inch Winchester disk could hold a hundred times as much as a normal floppy disk. It would also rotate about ten times faster.

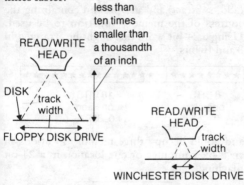

Sizes currently available include 5¼ inches, 8 inches and 14 inches; thus many micro-computer manufacturers offer a choice of Winchester or floppy disk drives with the same machine.

Word Many computers work with a fixed number of **bits** at a time and these are called words. The **memory** of such computers is also organised in words and the 'word-length' is measured by the number of bits each word contains.

For example: most **instructions** that operate the processor contain two parts, an operator (add, subtract) and an **operand** containing the address of the memory **location** to be used. Using a 24-bit word this might be arranged in 8 and 16 bits

★★★★★★★★	★★★★★★★★★★★★★★★★

    8 BITS   16 BITS
   operator   operand
   0–255   0–65535

and could occupy three memory locations in an 8-bit computer or one location in a 24-bit machine.

Word Processor This is a computer specifically used for the typing and production of letters, reports and documents. In addition to allowing corrections of a single **character** it will **justify** both right and left hand margins, centralise headings, move paragraphs, number pages, search for particular words and in some cases check spellings. Some manufacturers sell their machines as word processors; others offer word processing packages for particular com-

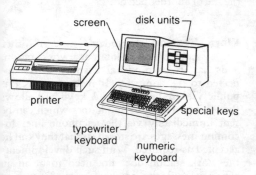

screen

disk units

printer

special keys

typewriter keyboard

numeric keyboard

puters. Although there are variations between
the different word processors (the number of
extra keys for example) the quality of the final
document depends on the type of **printer**.
Modern technology could replace the printer
with **electronic mail** whereby the text
created on one word processor is sent via the
telephone system to another office where it is
read from a screen and/or stored electronically.

For example: such a system allows the jottings
of one person to be inserted automatically into
the file of another person.

Work Station In today's modern office
one sits not just at a desk but at a work station.
This has its own **visual display unit** connected to the company's **database** as well as
public **viewdata** systems. A keyboard allows
the typing of memos and letters which can be
sent immediately via the telephone line. In-
coming messages are stored so that they can be
accepted as required. With such developments
the work station does not need to be in an
office; it could be on the factory floor or at
home.

Work Tape A magnetic tape which is available for use at any time. It might be used to hold the **data** in a sorting **routine** or the intermediate results of a long calculation.

Xerographic Printer This printer which prints a page at a time uses a dry copying process. The image is projected on to a light sensitive plate using a laser beam and the plate is covered with powder which is then transferred to paper. Such printers are capable of high speeds (20 pages per minute), good graphics (high resolution) and offer good colour but are expensive. Sometimes referred to as a 'xerographic laser printer' or just 'laser printer'.

X—Y Plotter An instrument for drawing lines on paper often used to draw the two-dimensional graphic output from a computer. On some instruments the pen is able to move in two directions; on others the pen moves in one direction and the paper is moved at right angles. Another method is to have the paper fixed to a cylinder which is able to revolve back and forwards whilst the pen moves sideways. Movement is generally done by **stepping motors**. Colour is achieved by using several (say four) different coloured pens, the carrier which moves selecting the right pen at the right time.

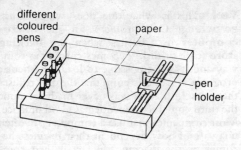

different coloured pens

paper

pen holder

Yell This is what one does when things go wrong. One problem for the **microcomputer** user occurs when the **backing store** (tape or disk) becomes corrupt in some way and it is not possible to load a particular program. It is at this point that the user realises that a **backup** copy was never made let alone the third copy recommended as good practice. Most companies that use a computer are often unaware of how dependent their business becomes on the machine. In fact if their computer system was put out of action completely most would find it difficult to survive. Hence the need for adequate insurance and backup facilities.

Zone　This generally refers to specific regions on a **punched card** as shown below but can refer to print positions.

For example: in **BASIC**, variables separated by semicolons are printed together whilst those separated by commas are printed in separate zones.

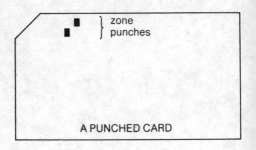

A PUNCHED CARD

Zone Refining　This is the method used to obtain a pure substance such as the **silicon** required for making **integrated circuits**. Starting at one end the material is melted and this molten zone is made to move along the sample to the other end. This is repeated several times always in the same direction and each time more of the impurities move with the molten zone to one end of the sample. In the case of silicon this pure substance is doped and then grown into a large cylindrical crystal (using a **seed crystal**) from which **wafers** are sliced.